FIGHTING WORDS

The Greatest Muhammad Ali Stories Ever Told

Edited by Keith McArthur

FanReads
Toronto, Canada

www.fanreads.com

Excerpts are reprinted with permission, detailed at the end of each selection.

First Edition

ISBN 978-1-988420-00-4 (paperback)
ISBN 978-1-988420-01-1 (electronic)

Cover by Inspired Cover Design
Book design by Keith McArthur

Printed and bound in Canada

FanReads Inc.
Suite #912
6A The Donway West
Toronto, Ontario M3C 2E8

www.fanreads.com
contact@fanreads.com

For Bryson, the greatest fighter I know.

CONTENTS

[Introduction]

By Keith McArthur

"Float like a butterfly, sting like a bee. Rumble, young man, rumble."

When Muhammad Ali died in June of 2016, the world mourned a saint who fought beautifully in the ring and sacrificed himself outside of it to stand up against inequality and unjust wars.

And that's part of who Ali was.

But that's not all he was. Muhammad Ali was a controversial figure, and to smooth out his rough edges is to miss much of the incredible narrative of Ali's life. It is to miss that Ali initially rejected Martin Luther King's vision of peaceful desegregation. It is to miss that Ali used hateful speech against his black opponents, attacking them for being Christian and "Uncle Toms." It is to miss that Ali held dangerous views, not just for the white status quo, but for the mainstream civil rights movement.

At his worst, he was mean, sexist and self-obsessed. At his best, he was a kind, generous man who loved to be around people, playing practical jokes and preaching peace and tolerance.

More words have been written about Muhammad Ali than perhaps any other athlete and this anthology cannot cover every side of

Cassius Clay / Muhammad Ali. Instead, I have collected some of the greatest stories that offer glimpses into Ali's life and why he mattered.

The first and longest part of the book includes stories from Ali's life in something close to chronological order. We hear from fighters he faced such as George Chuvalo and George Foreman and those he inspired such as James "Quick" Tillis. Ali's fight doctor Ferdie Pacheco takes us through the making of Ali's fictionalized fight against former heavyweight champion Rocky Marciano. Victor Bockris presents us with a snapshot of Ali the poet. And we read Davis Miller's remarkable first-person account of his night with Ali after Parkinson's disease was taking its toll on the champ. We also hear the story behind Ali's re-emergence at the 1996 Olympic Games.

To properly understand Ali, we also need to explore where he fit into the context of race and the civil rights movement in America. Michael Ezra argues that in his earliest years, Ali's story was framed in ways that made him more palatable to the white citizens of Louisville. Mike Marqusee explores Ali's controversial relationship with the Nation of Islam, its founder Elijah Muhammad and its most famous member Malcom X.

And of course, we hear from Ali himself in passages from his 1975 autobiography. First, Ali tells us the story of how he got into boxing in Louisville. Then we hear Ali's own words about his "Fight of the Century" against Joe Frazier. We've also included more recent reflections from Ali on why he refused the draft.

The book concludes with several reflections on the life Ali lived, as a boxer, as an activist and as America's most famous Muslim. We include President Barack Obama's tribute. And we include a piece that focuses on the most problematic years of Ali's life, from 1964 to 1975. During this period of time, Ali made controversial statements on the role of women, desegregation and race violence. His views began to change after 1975 when he converted from the Nation of Islam to the more mainstream Sunni Islam. Over time, his public statements evolved to better fit the Ali we like to remember now, as a tolerant ambassador for peace and equality.

The title of this book, *Fighting Words*, has multiple meanings.

Not only was Ali a fighter, he was a notorious trash talker, a practice he learned from wrestler "Gorgeous" George Wagner. He famously described Sonny Liston as stinky bear and vowed to take him home after the fight and make him into a rug. But Ali's fighting words outside of the ring were even more potent. His words about race in America and the war in Vietnam challenged the status quo and made him an enemy to many Americans.

Much of the history of the United States is the history of race, from slavery to the civil war to emancipation to desegregation to Black Lives Matter. As America's most famous athlete, Ali is an important part of this narrative.

Ali's story is so appealing because it is a classic redemption arc. He is a man who falls, goes into exile, and is reborn first as a hero and later as a saint. What makes his story special, however, is that it is bidirectional. When Ali lights the torch at the 1996 Olympic Games, it's not just that America is forgiving him for his past. Ali himself is forgiving his country.

[Timeline]

1942

- January 17: **Cassius Marcellus Clay Jr.** is born in Louisville, Kentucky.

1954

- Clay takes up boxing in a Louisville gym.

1960

- Clay wins the light-heavyweight gold medal at the Summer Olympics in Rome.
- October 29: Clay fights his first professional bout beating **Tunney Hunsaker**. Over the next three years, Clay goes 19–0 and earns himself a right to take on the world champion.

1962

- Clay quietly joins the Nation of Islam.

1964

- February 25: Clay becomes the heavyweight champion of the world when he beats **Sonny Liston** in a six-round upset. After the fight, he confirms publicly that he is part of the Nation of Islam. He changes his name to Muhammad Ali.
- June 4: Ali marries his first wife **Sonji Roi**. They divorce in 1966 after less than two years.

1966

- February 17: Ali publicly expresses his feelings about the war in Vietnam: "I ain't got no quarrel with them Viet Cong."
- March 29: Already a controversial figure because of his renunciation of the war in Vietnam, it becomes harder to find locations in the United States willing to host his fights. In Toronto, Canada, Ali fights **George Chuvalo** for the first time.

1967

- April 28: Ali is drafted for the US military but refuses. He is stripped of his World Boxing Association title and loses his license to fight. He is "in exile" from boxing for three years.
- June 25: Ali receives a five-year jail sentence for refusing to join the army. Imprisonment is put on hold pending appeals.
- August 17: Ali marries his second wife, seventeen-year-old **Belinda Boyd**. His bride converts to Islam and changes her name to **Khalilah Camacho-Ali**. They have four children together before divorcing in 1976.

1970

- August 11: Though his case is still under appeal, Ali is granted a license to box by the City of Atlanta Athletic Commission. The exile is officially over. On October 26, he returns to the ring to fight **Jerry Quarry** in Atlanta and knocks him out in the third round.

1971

- March 8: Dubbed the "Fight of the Century," Ali fights **Joe Frazier** for the first time. The fight goes the distance but Ali loses.
- June 28: The Supreme Court overturns Ali's conviction.
- July 26: Ali knocks out **Jimmy Ellis**, his hometown sparring partner from Louisville.

1973

- Ali loses to **Ken Norton**. It is only the second loss of his professional career, compared with forty-one wins. Ali will fight Norton two more times and wins both rematches.

1974

- January 28: Fight number two against **Joe Frazier**. Ali wins.
- October 30: Ali regains the heavyweight title when he knocks out **George Foreman** in the famed "Rumble in the Jungle" in Kinshasa, Zaire. It is here he meets **Veronica Porsche**, one of the poster girls who promoted the fight. They get married in 1977 and have two children together before divorcing in 1986.

1975

- October 1: Ali's third fight against **Joe Frazier** in the "Thrilla in Manila" in the Philippines. Ali retains his belt when Frazier can't come out for the fifteenth round.
- Ali converts from the Nation of Islam to the more mainstream Sunni Islam.

1978

- February 15: Ali loses the heavyweight title to **Leon Spinks** in a fifteen-round split decision.
- September 15: Ali goes fifteen rounds again against **Leon Spinks**. This time he comes out the winner, regaining the World Boxing Association version of the title. Ali is 36 years old.

1979

- July 27: Ali announces his retirement.

1980

- October 2: Ali comes out of retirement to fight **Larry Holmes** and loses badly.

1981

- December 11: One month before his 40th birthday, Ali gets into the ring for the last time, losing to Canadian **Trevor Berbick** in Nassau. This brings his career record to fifty-six wins and five losses.

1984

- Ali is diagnosed with Parkinson's disease.

1986

- Ali marries his fourth wife **Yolanda (Lonnie) Williams**. Fifteen years younger than Ali, they first met when she was only six years old.

1996

- July 19: Ali lights the Olympic cauldron at the Summer Games in Atlanta.

2015

- December 9: Ali issues a rare public statement on the subject of "Presidential Candidates Proposing to Ban Muslim Immigration to the United States."

2016

- June 3: Ali dies in Scottsdale, Arizona.

[PART ONE]

The Life of Muhummad Ali

FIGHTING WORDS

[ONE]

Tomorrow's Champions

By Muhammad Ali with Richard Durham

Muhammad Ali teamed up with Richard Durham to publish his autobiography in 1975. The book, edited by Nobel-prize winning novelist Toni Morrison, includes the account of Ali throwing his Olympic gold medal into the Ohio River after experiencing racism in his hometown Louisville. While it later came out that this story was not true, it continues to be a persistent component of the Ali myth and was prominent in many obituaries after Ali's death. In the following excerpt, Ali describes his formative years learning to box in Louisville. —Keith McArthur

~

The story that my boxing career began because my bike was stolen is a true one, as far as it goes. But that was only a part of it. I was twelve years old, and me and Johnny Willis, my closest buddy, had been out riding around on our bikes until the rain got too heavy. We were looking for something else to do when Johnny suddenly remembered seeing an ad for a black business exhibition at Columbia Auditorium on 4th and York. The auditorium is a big recreational center, with a boxing gym and a bowling alley. Every year the black people in the city hold a big bazaar, the Louisville Home Show, at the Columbia Gym.

At first I didn't want to go to the Home Show very much, but when we read the leaflet we saw that there would be free popcorn, free hot dogs and free candy. Besides, my father had bought me a new bike for Christmas, a Schwinn with red lights and chrome trim, a spotlight in the front, whitewall tires and chrome spokes and rims, and I wanted to show it off.

At the show we focused in on the food, and we hung around eating until seven o'clock, when everybody was leaving.

The rain was still coming down heavy as we left, so it took a while for us to notice that my bicycle was gone. Angry and frightened of what my father would do, we ran up and down the streets, asking about the bike. Someone told us to go downstairs to the Columbia Gym. "There's a policeman, Joe Elsby Martin, down there in the recreation center. Go and see him."

I ran downstairs, crying, but the sights and sounds and the smell of the boxing gym excited me so much that I almost forgot about the bike.

There were about ten boxers in the gym, some hitting the speed bag, some in the ring, sparring, some jumping rope. I stood there, smelling the sweat and rubbing alcohol, and a feeling of awe came over me. One slim boy shadowboxing in the ring was throwing punches almost too fast for my eyes to follow.

"You'll have to give me a report," Martin said calmly, and wrote down what I told him. Then, as I was about to go, he tapped me on the shoulder. "By the way, we got boxing every night, Monday through Friday, from six to eight. Here's an application in case you want to join the gym."

I was about 112 pounds, skinny, and I'd never had on a pair of boxing gloves. I folded up the paper and stuck it in my pocket, thinking it was a poor thing to take home instead of a bike. That night my father bawled me out for being so careless. And for once I was in total agreement with him. I told him I was sorry, and I meant it.

That Saturday I was home looking at a TV show called *Tomorrow's Champions*, an amateur boxing show, and there was the face of Joe Martin, working in the corner with one of his boys.

I nudged my mother. "Bird, that's the man I told about the bicycle. He wants me to come and box. Where's that application?"

She had taken the paper out of my pocket when she washed my clothes, but now she went and got it. "You want to be a boxer?" She was serious.

"I want to be a boxer," I said.

"How you going to get down there? It's a long way off. Your bike is gone. There's no carfare for that."

"Oh, I'll borrow somebody's bike," I said. "And I don't have nothin' else to do."

I remember my father looked uncertain. Then someone outside opened the door and yelled, "Johnny Willis's out here waiting for Cassius."

That decided it. "Well, boxing is better than running around with Willis and that gang," my father said. "Anything will beat that. Let him go."

When I got to the gym, I was so eager I jumped into the ring with some older boxer and began throwing wild punches. In a minute my nose started bleeding. My mouth was hurt. My head was dizzy. Finally someone pulled me out of the ring.

At that moment I was thinking I would be better off in the streets, but a slim welterweight came up and put his arms around my shoulders, saying, "You'll be all right. Just don't box these older fellows first. Box the fellows who are new like you. Get someone to teach you how to do it."

But there was hardly anybody to teach me anything. Martin knew a little. He could show me how to place my feet and how to throw a right cross, but he knew very little else. I was fighting like a girl, throwing wild, loopy punches. But something was driving me and

I kept fighting and I kept training. And although I still roamed the streets with the gang, I kept coming back to the gym.

"I like what you're doing," Martin said to me one day. "I like the way you stick to it. I'm going to put you on television. You'll be on the next television fight."

Thrilled at the idea of being seen on TV all over Kentucky, I trained the whole week. They matched me with a white fighter, Ronny O'Keefe, and I won my first fight by a split decision.

All of a sudden I had a new life. Inside the gang, I was getting recognition as a fighter. My father walked up and down Boston Street after my first victory, predicting, "My son is going to be another Joe Louis. The World Heavyweight Champion, Cassius Clay." Bird began to see how I resembled Louis. "Hasn't he got a big round head like Joe Louis?" she asked my cousins.

And from then on she would recall how I used to jump up in the bed and say, "GG." "Those were the only things he could understand. The two letters, GG." And I would make the joke about how I was trying to tell her I was going to be a Golden Gloves Champion.

Even the gap in her two front teeth, she would now attribute to me. "When he was a baby he had the fighting instinct in him. I was spanking him and he got mad and swung at me and knocked both of my two front teeth out of place. He was only a year old then. It shows how hard he could hit from the start."

And each week Joe Martin would book me on *Tomorrow's Champions* because in the ring I flailed away, even after I was exhausted, and I was winning. Not because I was so skilled but because I never stopped. The other fighters would go down or quit or get discouraged.

But it was while fighting in my first Kentucky State Golden Gloves tournament that I learned more from a defeat than from all the victories I had been accumulating under Martin. In that tournament, a black fighter beat me decisively. I was hurt, but I knew I had been beaten by a better boxer and I knew where he came from. Grace Community Center, a boxing gym over in the all-black part of town, under the guidance of a trainer named Fred Stoner.

I had already noticed that the boys from Stoner's gym were

better boxers than those at Martin's. They were counterpunchers, with better rhythm. Their timing was better, their punches sharper.

Martin's strict rule was that there be no association with Stoner. I was getting four dollars every time I boxed on *Tomorrow's Champions*, and Martin would not allow Stoner's boys to box on the show. Most of Martin's boys were white, and most of those he tried to seriously recruit were white.

One evening, watching Stoner's fighters outclass and outstyle boxers that had come in from another state for an exhibition, I was so impressed that I decided to take the chance. With Rudy, I walked all the way up to Grace Community Center and went down into the basement gym and met Stoner.

A slightly built, quiet black man, he was very intent in his work, watching every move his boxers made. I looked around. He didn't have the facilities that Joe Martin had. In the winter the basement of his church would be cold, while it was warm in Martin's gym. And his handbags and equipment were inferior to Martin's.

"If you want to come in, come on," he said.

"Have you seen me on TV?" I asked.

He nodded, unimpressed. "You got courage," he said. "You got the will, but you don't have the skill. We train here at night from eight to twelve o'clock. If you can get here, I'll show you how to fight."

The next morning, when I walked into the Columbia Gym, Joe Martin called me aside. "I heard you were over there training with Fred Stoner."

For some reason, I was frightened. He talked to me as though I had done something criminal.

"You know the rules in this gymnasium," he said. "No one can be with Stoner and be with me. It's up to you. Either drop Stoner or I'll drop you."

I felt my heart sinking. I needed the four dollars I was getting for boxing under Martin, but I also needed the science and skill Stoner was teaching. All of the black professionals—Jerome Dawson, Billy Williams, Bill Hestor, Green Gresham and Rudolph Stitch—had been molded by Stoner.

I remember standing in front of Martin, sweating and feeling degraded. I agreed to stay away from Stoner's gym.

But that year Fred Stoner's boys went to Chicago and brought back most of the amateur titles. They were beautiful fighters. Boxers. They had sharp hooks and they danced. They could jab, hit, move. They had pretty footwork. They could duck and weave. Some were even younger than I was, but their bodies looked mature. How did they get their bodies that way? I had to find out.

I remember one hot Saturday morning, making the long walk from 32nd Street to the gym on 6th Street where the boxers for *Tomorrow's Champions* assemble. I'm thirteen years old. I stop on 18th Street to watch boys and girls splashing around in a big swimming pool. As I stand there, a skinny boy in ragged tennis shoes, holding an old pair of dirty underwear-looking trunks, comes up next to me. I hold on to my own black and white striped trunks and we look each other over carefully.

"Where you going?" he asks, eyes on my trunks.

"I box today," I tell him.

"Who you fighting?"

"I don't know. I'm supposed to fight on a show, *Tomorrow's Champions*."

"That's funny. Me too."

"Who you fighting?"

"I don't know," he says.

And then a friend of his comes up on a bike, and he gets on and rides off to the gym, ahead of me.

By the time I get there, he's coming out the door, and he pushes me and says gruffly, "Well, you won't fight today." I rush over to find Joe Martin, and he points to the same boy and says, "That's the fellow you're supposed to fight, Jimmy Ellis, but he don't weigh enough."

I walk over to him. "You Jimmy Ellis?"

"You Cassius Clay?"

"Why don't you gain some weight," I say, as if being skinny is his fault. Tears are in his eyes. "We both lost four dollars because you're too skinny."

"We lost four dollars because you're too heavy!" he shoots back. "You're too young to weigh that much."

I can see he feels as bad as I do. I am two years younger than Jimmy, but I am also heavier. Later, we will fight even in an amateur tournament. He'll win one and I'll win one and we joke of someday fighting to break the tie. When I become Louisville's first World Heavyweight Champion, I will use Ellis as my main sparring partner. When I am stripped of the title, he will win the WBA's Heavyweight Elimination Tournament and be recognized by them as the World Heavyweight Champion. For a while little Louisville will have produced two Heavyweight Champions in a decade. And only when I am climbing back into contention, do we fight our final "rubber match," to break the tie.

It will come in Houston. He is the first fighter I face after my loss to Joe Frazier. And it's crucial that I beat him to prove I can come back. It's crucial for him to prove that he's more than just my sparring partner, but a real champion. A defeat by Ellis would mean extinction for me. Fortunately, I was always a little heavier and better than Jimmy.

By the end of that year, I knew I wanted to be a fighter. I decided to go down to Grace Community Center and learn the science of it, even if it meant cutting off a good source of income.

After school I would go to work four hours for the Catholic sisters, then train at Martin's gym from six to eight in the evening. From there I would go to get the real training at Stoner's gym from eight to twelve at night.

The discipline in Fred's gym was tough. Roadwork was like religion, and Fred was relentless in making me develop certain muscles which he believed were necessary for survival in the ring. He made us shoot left jabs, two hundred straight, sharp left jabs at a time without stopping. If we got tired, he made us start all over and count to a hundred, one, two, three ... shooting jabs until we could do the two hundred without feeling it. Then he made us shoot and jab and a right cross. Then come back with a hook, jab, left hook and duck; a jab and back up, a jab and move forward. He taught us to block, to shoot right crosses, and we went over it again and again. We did a hundred push-ups and a hundred knee bends.

In Martin's gym, all that was required was to punch the bag, jump ropes and jump in the ring and flail away at each other. All the publicity about my boxing origin and the early development of my boxing skill describes Joe Martin as the incubator. But my style, my stamina, my system were molded down in the basement of a church in East End.

I am fourteen years old, riding my little two-horsepower motor scooter. I am coming home in the rain from the basement gym at Grace Community Center in the East End of Louisville. I have been there all afternoon with Fred Stoner.

It begins to rain harder and I am driving, head down, zipping past parked cars until I pass one with its radio up loud and hear a roaring crowd. I put on the brakes, skid around and come back to hear more. A heavyweight boxing match is taking place. The car is too crowded for me to get in, but they let me put my head inside so I can hear. I have gotten there just in time to hear the announcer crying out above the noise, "And still the Heavyweight Champion of the World, Rocky Marciano!"

A cold chill shoots through my bones. I have never heard anything that affected me like those words: "Heavyweight Champion of the World." All the world? And from that day on I want to hear that said about me.

I pull my head out of the car and stand there in the rain. "Still Heavyweight Champion of the World, Cassius Clay!" I get back on my scooter and ride on, hearing that announcer's voice coming through the wind: "And still Heavyweight Champion of the World, Gene Tunney, Joe Louis, Ezzard Charles, Rocky Marciano, Floyd Patterson . . . Cassius Clay!"

I start dreaming: I can see myself telling my next-door neighbor,

"I'm getting ready to fight for the Heavyweight Title of the World!" And coming back the next night to say, "I'm now the Heavyweight Champion of the World!" The rain is cold and pouring down harder, and I ask myself, "Can I?" At this time I can't even beat everybody in my own gym. I ask Jim Martin. He shakes his head doubtfully. "You hardly weigh a hundred and fifteen pounds soaking wet. You know how big a heavyweight is? Maybe you could be a lightweight."

But I want "heavyweight." Somehow, although no one on either side of my family is that big, I feel I will be. I turn from him, and the next day I start training in earnest. I start watching fights on TV with more interest. What catches my eye is the way fighters trade punches with each other. I see Ralph "Tiger" Jones, Hurricane Jackson, Carmen Basilio, Gene Fullmer, and watch how they stand, and get hit with the same punch. Or jab each other over and over. And I know I can beat them. Even when I see Patterson. Even when I see Archie Moore. I know that one day I will be able to whip these men very easily, because they are not moving, not circling. Not moving backwards at the right time. I know I can learn to hit without getting hit. And every day in the gym I practice pulling back from the punches. I jab and then lean back. I learn that you can't dodge most punches by weaving, bobbing and ducking—not from short range.

Professionals around the gym tell me, "Someday you're going to get your head knocked off." But the wiser ones remember that Jack Johnson also leaned back.

Soon I develop a built-in radar. I know how far I can go back, when it's time to duck or time to tie my man up. I learn there is a science to making your opponent wear down. I learn to put my head within hitting range, force my opponent to throw blows, then lean back and away, keeping eyes wide open so I can see everything, then sidestep, move to the right, or to the left, jab him again, then again, put my head back in hitting range. It takes a lot out of a fighter to throw punches that land in the thin air. When his best combinations hit nothing but space, it saps him.

Throughout my amateur days, old boxers think I'm easy to hit, but I'm not. I concentrate on defense. I concentrate on timing and motions and pulling back. When I throw a jab, I know my opponent will throw a punch, and I pull back.

"I'm going to train harder," I told Stoner one night. "I want to know everything you can teach me."

Stoner was looking me hard in the eye, as if to see how serious I was. Then he said, "You're quick and you got the talent. Some of the best pros in the country are in town now. You get down to business, and when they hold the tournament in the fall, you will come out a champion."

A minute earlier my hands had been burning, my arms and legs aching, but what Stoner said was healing them faster than all the alcohol and iodine he had poured over them.

"You think I can win the Golden Gloves?"

"Not only the Golden Gloves, you'll take the Olympic Gold Medal in Rome." Stoner said it as though it was inevitable.

I had been winning most of my matches without much coaching, but after Stoner's lessons I was certain I would defeat my opponents. In 161 amateur fights out of 167, I did.

Both Martin and Stoner kept the gold of the Olympic Medal shining in my eyes: "It's worth a million dollars to a fighter. When you win that, you're a national hero. You're celebrated like Lindbergh. And the governor, the mayor, the police, even the President honors you. It's something you'll remember for the rest of your life."

They were right. I remember winning the Golden Gloves tournaments and the AAU titles. But what I remember most is the summer of 1960, when I came home from Rome to a hero's welcome.

~

[TWO]

Louisville's Favorite Son

By Michael Ezra

Cassius Clay's coming of age as a fighter coincided with the civil rights movement's coming of age in America. In this excerpt, Michael Ezra, Chair of the American Multicultural Studies Department at Sonoma State University, argues that Cassius Clay's story was initially framed in ways that made white Louisville more willing to embrace a young black hero. —K.M.

You've heard the story. A youngster goes into a merchandise fair in his hometown Louisville and parks his new Schwinn bicycle against a nearby wall. When he returns, the bike is missing. The agitated boy finds the nearest policeman and vows to beat up the culprit. The cop offers to teach the lad how to box. The kid becomes one of history's greatest fighters.

Twelve-year-old Cassius Marcellus Clay Jr. took up boxing in 1954, several months after the Supreme Court issued the landmark

Brown v. Board of Education verdict, which ordered public schools to be desegregated and thus jump-started the civil rights movement. Told and retold by virtually everyone who has chronicled his life as if it were one of its central events, the origin narrative pairing young Clay with policeman Joe Martin, his first amateur trainer, has become one of the seedbeds in which his cultural image has flourished. It is wrong to assume that the genesis of Clays amateur boxing career would necessarily become a cornerstone of the Ali Story. Its rising to such prominence is an important clue as to how people have made meaning of the legendary figure now known as Muhammad Ali. It is the first tale of the Ali mythology.

Prior to 1960, when Clay won the Olympic gold medal and achieved national recognition, his fame was local. Once he was introduced to a wider audience, interest in Clay's backstory developed. The young fighter's relationship with Martin, and then his business agreement with the Louisville Sponsoring Group (LSG), became the focus of coverage meant to acquaint people with him. Both Martin and the members of the LSG were white. Martin was a cop, a source of great displeasure to Clay's father, who had had his share of minor run-ins with the police. The LSG was made up of old-moneyed aristocrats who used Clay's career for sport and investment. What is critical here is that the earliest presentations of Clay to a national audience featured his ties to Martin and the LSG, and observers made sense of Clay's essential character and standing within American culture based upon the racial composition of these alliances. Early in his public life, Clay's acceptability emanated from his ties to white people.

The civil rights movement was a key reason that these narratives, both in their packaging and consumption, became central to the tradition of telling Cassius Clay's story. By the time Clay made his professional debut, the civil rights movement was changing life in the South. The movement generated support—although its halcyon days of public approval wouldn't come until a few years late—but it also engendered bitterness and resentment. The passion it produced made the black freedom struggle the leading domestic story of the period, and it could be seen and heard all over the cultural landscape.

The sit-in movement and its spawning of the vanguard Student Nonviolent Coordinating Committee (SNCC) were the two most important civil rights developments of 1960, the year Clay first achieved national recognition. Led by teenagers and people in their twenties, particularly college students, the sit-in movement rippled through places that had held fast to segregation. It started in February in North Carolina, when four protesters sat down at the white-only lunch counter at a Woolworth's store in Greensboro. News of their courage spread like wildfire, and by the middle of the month, young people throughout the state, as well as in South Carolina, Tennessee, and Virginia, had taken similar stands.

Most impressive about the sit-in movement was how it marshaled participation by young black people who wanted to be a part of the civil rights struggle. Coordinated by SNCC, sit-ins gripped nearly the entire South by the end of the year, even in places like Alabama, Mississippi, and Louisiana. As these campaigns grew stronger, owners of segregated businesses began to feel the economic pinch. They had to worry about disruptions in day-to-day activity, negative press coverage, and threats of violence against protesters. Targeted storeowners met the dilemma of having to either resist the demonstrators and face legal action or capitulate to them and face the wrath of segregationists. That showdown after showdown was featured in the media only escalated tensions.

White resistance took on many forms, the most spectacular and deadly occurring when people assaulted demonstrators, often with the blessing of local law enforcement. There were those who formalized their resistance and joined organizations like the Ku Klux Klan, blew things up, burned crosses, and shot people. Many others simply showed up at local sit-ins to make life tough for protesters when the opportunity presented itself. Resistance turned sit-ins into mob scenes, and black participants were often at great peril. There were also those white people, constituting the largest group of resisters, who just stayed home and watched television, shaking their heads and questioning why blacks were so angry.

As an eighteen-year-old southern black arriving on the national scene, Cassius Clay faced pressure to understand and articulate himself in relation to the civil rights movement. By the time he turned professional, the black freedom struggle was firmly entrenched in the news and culture and influenced how people understood who he was. In calculating how his public persona would affect his professional life, particularly his ability to make money, Clay and his advisers had to estimate how best to respond to these developments. Such consideration went back to Clays amateur days, when a Soviet reporter at the Olympics asked him about racial discrimination in the United States, and Clay scored points with his answer: "We got qualified people working on that problem, and I'm not worried about the outcome."

Throughout his amateur and early professional days, Clay developed a knack for coming up with the right answers during troubled times. Some people found him obnoxious, but mostly he was recognized as a good kid. Even at his most controversial, Clay enjoyed a special relationship with his hometown of Louisville, Kentucky, one characterized by mildness. Clay had what could be described as a typical working-class upbringing. He grew up in the predominantly black West End of the city. Less than a quarter mile to the east of the family home lay tracks belonging to the Kentucky and Indiana Terminal Railroad Company. A little farther in the opposite direction ran U.S. Highway 60, which had recently been incorporated into the interstate system. He wasn't necessarily on the wrong side of the tracks, although he was close to them. But there was always something to eat, presents at Christmas, and decent clothes. His mother Odessa worked as a maid, and his father Cassius Sr. made a living as a sign painter and commercial artist. With both parents present, he grew up in a private house, and he finished high school. In comparison to that of other heavyweight champions, Clay's upbringing was comfortable.

There is no doubt that Louisville endorsed Cassius Clay, as there is no doubt that he experienced frustrations growing up in a city that did not desegregate its public accommodations until the middle of 1963. Clay's father was outspoken about the foibles of white people, holding racism responsible for his inability to advance further as an artist and frequently lecturing young Cassius and his little brother Rudy about the pitfalls of growing up black in America. Although in reality it often typified the injustices of a segregated racial order, in the early days Clay's story would be framed in ways that uplifted white Louisville and assuaged its doubts about the civil rights movement. Clay's standing as the city's major-league sports franchise and a municipal representative held fast throughout his first few years as a professional fighter.

Locals initially took notice of Clay because of his boxing ability. Winning the gold medal in the light-heavyweight division at the 1960 Rome Olympics made front-page headlines in his hometown. Clay had lived his entire life in Louisville, and he was known to many city dwellers, especially sports fans, prior to the Olympics. He had already won national titles at the two most important amateur boxing tournaments, the Golden Gloves and the Amateur Athletic Union. But even before that, he was recognizable to many residents as the talkative, spindly kid who had been seen a bunch of times on the local television program *Tomorrow's Champions*, for which he received four dollars per appearance. Joe Martin's connections gave Clay access to the show.

Although he often trained as an amateur with a black man named Fred Stoner, far more people know about Clay's relationship with Martin. There are several explanations floating around about the entanglements between the boxer and his two trainers. One is that Stoner kicked Clay out of his gym for failing to listen to instruction. Another is that Clay hid his relationship with Stoner so that Martin would not get upset and ban him from the television show. The most popular version of the story paints a friendly relationship between Clay and Martin while leaving Stoner out altogether. In the early days of Clay's career, it was critical that people recognized Joe Martin as his trainer because it produced the governing sentiment that the young man had to be OK if his mentor was a white cop. This was no small thing in a southern city during the tense early days of the civil rights movement.

It wasn't what Clay said or didn't say that made him an accessible symbol, but the way he appeared to approach life. He seemed simple enough: a clean-living kid who avoided trouble and wanted to become a boxer for the right reasons, namely to make money. The corniness of local coverage surrounding Clay's Olympic victory testifies to the wholesomeness of his image at the time. A big story centered on the giant turkey dinner his parents planned for his return to town, and articles played up, wrongfully, his quiet and unassuming manner. "I'm the onliest champion in the world that's got nothing jingling in his jeans," he said. "Just as soon as I can find me a manager with some money, I'm turning pro." Boxing one day would become Clay's vehicle to historical status beyond what anyone could have expected, but at the time of his turning professional, it was simply a means to become rich. It was what he excelled at, and it potentially paid very well.

There was also a sense that Clay didn't really have what it took to shake things up beyond the ring. His academic profile was limited. He withdrew from high school near the end of tenth grade after making horrendous grades but returned the following year. He never fulfilled Central High School's graduation requirements, but the principal insisted that he pass anyway. "One day our greatest claim to fame is going to be that we knew Cassius Clay or taught him," Atwood Wilson told faculty. "Do you think I'm going to be the principal of a school that Cassius Clay didn't finish? Why, in one night, he'll make more money than the principal and all you teachers make in a year." The matter was settled. Clay would be ranked 376th out of 391 graduating seniors, receiving not a diploma but the minimum recognition, a certificate of attendance, for his efforts. Anyone familiar with his story could have easily thought that he was kind of stupid, his quick-witted outbursts notwithstanding.

The icing on Clay's cake of acceptability came in Rome, when he told the Soviet reporter who had grilled him on race relations, "To me the U.S.A. is the best country in the world, including yours." It wasn't just high white society that was pleased. The local black weekly, the *Louisville Defender*, called him "an ambassador of goodwill... with his stark honest interpretation of U.S. race conditions." Clay's whole package was one that all of Louisville could appreciate. Amid the torrent of nationwide racial unrest, Clay's friendship with a white cop and lack of scholarly ambition were sources of relief.

Combined with the real achievement of winning a gold medal, these narratives led to an enormous reception for Clay, one that might normally be reserved for a visiting head of state, when he returned to Louisville from the Olympics. First there was the airport reception, as about 200 people, including politicians, cheerleaders, friends, and family packed Standiford Field to meet him, letting out a roar when the plane touched down. Once he got his bearings, there was a television interview alongside Mayor Bruce Hoblitzell, who congratulated the young man on behalf of the city. Then a fifty-car motorcade led Clay down Walnut Street, renamed Muhammad Ali Boulevard some two decades later, toward Central High School, where Louisville's leading citizens joined the rank and file for a celebration.

At the assembly, Congressman Frank W. Burke told the audience that Clay "has brought honor not only to his school but to Louisville and all of Jefferson County. We have great pride in him for his accomplishments. This is only one of several steps that will lead him higher in his field of endeavor." Despite Clay's academic past, a procession of teachers, students, administrators, and principals lauded him. "You just can't beat success," said William Chilton, Louisville's assistant superintendent of schools. "I wish to honor Clay personally for his ability to get to the top. This is a great honor for the entire school system." Around town, people from all walks of life feted young Cassius. Neighbourhood improvement groups presented him with certificates. He sang at the Kentucky State Fair. *The Louisville Defender* bought into the triage, describing him as "intensely happy," "humble," "unassuming," and "awed." He was Louisville's favorite son, seemingly endorsed by the entire city.

Then came Clay's professional debut, which from a promotional standpoint was different from any other in his career. Because it stands apart from the rest of his bouts, and requires an explanation all its own, there is an utter lack of coverage of the match in the Ali literature. This is disappointing because it is a critical indicator of the young fighter's cultural image at the start of his professional career and of the commercial benefits he stood to reap as a result of it. A slice of Americana wrapped in red, white, and blue bunting, Clay's professional send-off was marked by pageantry and righteousness. Few boxing matches enjoyed the authoritative backing that this one had.

Fueled by a peculiar combination of civic pride, ego, political opportunism, philanthropy, and integrationist belief, a coalition of Louisville elites, spearheaded by Mayor Hoblitzell and consisting of the city's business leaders, politicians, boxing insiders, and community groups, planned Clay's professional debut. Although he had yet to hire a managerial team, Clay had been adopted, if you will, by bigwigs who made it their business to make sure that his career got off on the right foot.

Mayor Hoblitzell and automobile dealer Wood Hannah, with the cooperation of Bill King, the city's leading boxing promoter, hatched a plan to start Clay's career right and "put a little money in the kid's pocket." It would take place October 26 at the State Fairgrounds, and proceeds would benefit the nearby Kosair Crippled Children Hospital. Clay would receive a $2,000 purse, which for a professional debut was outstanding. The *Louisville Courier-Journal* called it "very generous" and a "terrific payday," while the *Defender* referred to it as "quite a chunk of money for a fellow in his first fight."

With the mayor and other powerful citizens behind this benefit for a children's hospital, Clay's debut seemed as much a good deed as a sporting event. It indicated that great spoils went along with being admired. Clay's moral authority, his being the right kind of symbol, stood to benefit him financially. His debut was an early indication of the linkages between cultural image and commercial viability. Nationwide civil rights unrest and a burgeoning student movement intensified the power of this connection.

Not just elites, but large segments of the community got involved. Local media treated the fight as a major event. Half-page newspaper ads, accompanied by a full-body picture of Clay in fighting togs, implored readers to "HELP A CRIPPLED CHILD WALK!" How could you not want to get involved in something like that? Kroger, the grocery chain with seventy-one area stores, sold tickets and provided free parking for the event. An executive for the franchise told *Louisville Courier-Journal* reporter Clarence Royalty that the corporation wanted "to give Clay an excellent start in his pro career and to do something for the Kosair Crippled Children Hospital." Through direct solicitations, business leaders canvassed their friends and sold 1,500 top-priced seats. Wilma Rudolph, three-time Olympic gold medalist and student at nearby Tennessee A&I, was brought in to generate interest. Governor Bert Combs waived the State Fairgrounds rental fee. Two weeks before the bout, *Courier-Journal* sports editor Earl Ruby reported that promoter Bill King had found an opponent capable of letting Cassius know that he's no longer meeting amateurs." Tunney Hunsaker, the Kentucky native who had become the police chief of Fayetteville, West Virginia, would face the Olympic star in a six-rounder. Hunsaker, who received $250 plus $100 expense money, was experienced and game but little else. He sported a 13–9 record and had taken on contenders like Bert Whitehurst, who twice went the distance with the fearsome Sonny Liston; Tom McNeeley, who had lost a championship match to Floyd Patterson; and a young Chicago prospect named Ernie Terrell, who had beaten him by decision.

About six weeks after returning from Rome, Clay debuted amid what Bob Weston of the *Louisville Times* called "probably the greatest fanfare ever drummed up for a six-round bout." The fight itself was one of both disappointment and promise, of criticism and praise, of failure and success. About 6,000 people paid over $12,000, an extremely impressive amount for such an event, to see a closed-circuit telecast of a welterweight bout from New York, a pair of four-round scraps involving inexperienced local pros, and the main event between Clay and Hunsaker. Such gate receipts portended a potentially huge windfall to whoever won the sweepstakes to manage the Olympic champion. Clay earned a unanimous-decision victory, becoming the first heavyweight champion in nearly thirty-five years (James J. Braddock) not to win by knockout in his first pro bout. Clay took the match decisively, closing Hunsaker's right eye and bloodying his nose. Even so, some fans booed near the end of the contest, and local sportswriters were not impressed. The charity arm of the show was also something of a letdown. Expenses ran higher than expected, the closed-circuit broadcast cost over $2,300 to air, and the Kosair Crippled Children Hospital received only $2,500 from the benefit. "This didn't come close to what we expected," said a spokesperson for the mayor's committee. Despite the imperfections, however, things basically went according to plan. Clay received a nice purse and got some experience. Louisville got a boxing show and a chance to celebrate a local hero. The Children Hospital got a check. Most important, Clay was firmly aligned with Louisville's elite. With their economic clout and perceived moral authority behind him, he was ready to move on to bigger and better things.

Excerpt from "Louisville's Favorite Son: The Professional Debut" from Muhammad Ali: The Making of an Icon by Michael Ezra. Used by permission of Temple University Press.

[THREE]

"I Wanna Be Cassius Clay"

By James "Quick" Tillis as told to J. Engleman Price

Ali inspired countless boxers. In the following account, seven-year-old James Tillis watches Cassius Clay defeat Sonny Liston to win the heavyweight title for the first time. Tillis himself would challenge for the title in the eighties. He is best known as the first man to go the distance against Mike Tyson. The excerpt begins 33 years after he first watched Ali fight when Tillis began writing his autobiography from a jail cell. —K.M.

~

The fat red and brown roaches crawled between the bars of my cell that month, beggin for some of the stale Rainbow bread I'd have at dinner. I was tryin to get that sick pee smell outta my nose. *Could be worse.* I looked around. Black dudes, white dudes, Mexican dudes, some in for murderin their wives, some for stealin $400 from QuikTrip for a day of crack.

A bunch of losers and quitters, just hopin to get out one day, maybe even get a real job with benefits and stuff, get a house with a backyard instead of lookin out of some run-down apartment with concrete and yellow lines for a yard. Yeah, they'd get out, all right, but without that needle or bottle or gun, they'd be right back in, back in the can with me.

They'd taken my teeth. I couldn't even smile at nothin. I DON'T BELONG HERE. *Get me outta this orange suit, don't make me walk outside like some crazy animal with cuffs around my legs and wrists. I'm not like the rest of these losers. I'm not a quitter.*

Sure, who'd believe me? I'd made a quarter million in a few years fightin the best. I'd made the champions wish they'd put someone else in the corner. I'd had my name printed on flashy handbags and jackets, on the Bronco that I paid for in cash. I'd been all over the world, been in the movies, ate dinner with MOOOvie stars. Never drank, never smoked, never did drugs. Yeah, I was different. I was rottin in a Tulsa jail cell for sendin my $100-a-month child-support checks to the wrong address; I was sendin 'em, she was never gettin 'em. So the judge told me, "get your ass in that six by-six cell," where I sat writin my story, gettin my pencils sharpened a few times a day by guys wantin to help out a heavyweight contender.

It had all started 33 years ago, one night in 1964 …

The old black and white sat where it always sat, on that damn linoleum floor. Kids with snotty noses gobbled down Mamas greasy collard greens and stale cornbread, some aunts and uncles argued about who was gonna watch what. Then Mama took off her apron and looked for an empty spot on the couch—a hard thing to do with seven children. The Tillis family waited for the magic to begin.

"And now, LAAAAdies and gentleman, the two contenders of the evening. The infamous Sonny Liston, HEAAAAAvy-weight CHAMpion of the world. In the other corner, CAAAAASSSSSSIUS CLAAAAY."

The Miami men with them suntans on their faces and their fat, smelly cigars screamed from the TV audience, "KILL HIM, Sonny. Make 'im feel it!"

The proud champion moved around in his corner like he owned the world, shadowboxin the air like he'd already won or somethin.

Clay, the young 22-year-old kid, also shadowboxed in his own corner, but this kid was dancin. A heavyweight dancin on air? No way.

Cassius Clay. I'd heard about this boxer and seen some pictures of him in *Sports Illustrated* at school. But I'd never seen him on television. When I watched him makin moves with his feet like some nervous kid at his first school dance, I had this weird feelin. Somethin was about to happen, I just didn't know what. I could feel it in my blood, real warm like, like it was me doin the fightin.

But I was just a seven-year-old kid, who went to school most days, except when I fooled Mama by fakin a cough or pretendin to have a stomachache. Couldn't fake out Mama too much, though. She knew her two sons and five daughters better than anybody's business, like a mother hen knows every one of her chicks. You couldn't fool Mama.

If I wasn't tryin to skip school, I was out chasin the neighbor girls or stealin other boys' bicycle parts, like the handlebars or the padded seats. I was a bad little boy. I used to walk right up to some eight-year-old boy who was bigger than me, hit him in the face with my scrawny, dirty fist, and then run like hell, hidin behind the closest thing I could find, usually my oldest sister, Glenda.

"Get your paws off my little brother!" she'd yell like those lions I'd heard at the Tulsa Zoo. My troubles were solved . . . for a while.

After three or four times of me runnin through the broken porch door hollerin for someone to save me, Mama put a stop to the fist-fights with one good twig from the biggest willow in our front yard and one good buck-naked ass.

I didn't even want to watch no boxing match that night. I wanted to throw the football around with a few of my neighbor friends—it really didn't matter that it was 28 degrees and the middle of February.

But somethin crawled into the drafty old house that winter night of 1964. I call it the Spirit of God. I call it God's will. Because of it, I'd never be the same.

"I am the greatest! I'm gonna put that ugly bear on the floor and after the fight I'm gonna build myself a pretty home and use him as a bearskin rug. Liston even smells like a bear."

I loved these strange words comin out of this good-lookin black athlete's mouth. It was a confidence and a teasin that I hadn't seen from a fighter before, specially a black man. He was playin with Liston like some kid's toy—teasin, teasin, never backin off, even though he didn't have no chance.

"It's gonna go so far down his throat," Liston bragged about his left fist, "that it'll take a week for me to pull it out again." We believed him. We'd seen what Liston could do with Floyd "The Rabbit" Patterson and "Big Cat" Cleveland Williams.

So who was this other black guy on the screen claimin to be the greatest? He was gettin ready to step into the ring with a heavyweight monster who'd beaten the crap out of plenty of fighters.

Ding. Round one. "And Clay steps toward Liston . . . " Somethin about that fight pulled me in, like I couldn't see nothin else, like some magician was workin a trance on me, drawin my eyes to Clay's every move. The feet, so quick and full of life, flyin in the air like those hummingbirds I'd seen outside my living-room windows in the summer. His quick jabs that I'd miss if I blinked, his head movement, side to side dodgin Liston's left jab, and another, and another.

"I wanna be like him, Jerry," I heard my voice say to my step father, just kinda whisperin. But nobody paid me no attention. Jerry just kept his eyes glued on the set, boxin in the air once in a while, Mama tried to get some sewin done on my brother's bluejeans, and my five sisters were punchin at each other. 'Get 'im, Clay. Knock that sucka out, Clay!" Jerry yelled.

"I wanna . . . " I tried again.

You what?" asked Mama with her gentle smile.

"I wanna be . . ."

"THAT A WAY, CLAY! GO FOR THE JAW!"

"I can't believe what we're seeing can you? No one expected anyone to look so good against Liston," exclaimed the commentators.

"I . . . I . . . "

"CLAY'S THE MAN! CLAY'S THE MAN!"

"I . . . wanna . . . I wanna . . . I wanna be LIKE HIM! I WANNA BE CASSIUS CLAY!" I yelled at the top of my lungs, arms spread high above my head, the white baby teeth still in my mouth shinin like a toothpaste commercial.

"All, go awn and sit yourself down, Junior," scolded my sister Glenda. "I can't see with you squawkin and jumpin around like that."

"That's nice," said Mama. "You can be whoever you want to be. Just be quiet now so we can all watch the fight."

I knew nobody thought I was really serious. Sure, little kids think lots of things. They want to be cowboys, cops, firemen. Some want to be just like Daddy, if they have one. But that night Clay kept me from gettin discouraged. If he could do it, I could do it.

The fight kept goin. Round two, round three, round four, with the Tillises huddled close to Liston's and Clay's every black-and-white move. Clay movin clockwise around the ring, Liston hittin Clay with a body shot, a left in the ribs, a forceful jab at the face. But even with Liston's reputation of bein able to actually lift a fighter off the ground with his left jab, he couldn't get close to Clay.

Round five. Blood smeared along Liston's jaw, Vaseline and slimy snot mixed together under his nose and ran down his chin. Clay's shiny muscles wrapped around Liston exhausted but determined. Liston was gettin beat.

I knew, as I stared at the man not many people believed in, that I wasn't alone. I had Cassius Clay on my side. I didn't have to be no black man who picked up his food stamps every month or died at 19 from a neighborhood bullet in his head. I wasn't gonna be like my friends who were just gonna do little things because they thought little. I was thinkin big things now and I knew who was on my side—Cassius Clay and God Almighty.

Ding. Round six. A left hook into Liston's head. BAM, BAM. Another. Liston's soggy mouthpiece flew through the air like one of them white flags in the war movies I seen on television, surrenderin. The fight was over.

Liston fell on his stool, his cornerman by his side. "No more, no more," he told the man rubbin him down. "No more . . . . I quit."

The crowds at the fight were shocked. Their boy, Sonny Liston, beaten by some cocky jerk who claimed to be the king of the world.

Clay couldn't have been more alive, even though he'd just gone six rounds with the heavyweight champion of the world.

"I'm the king of the woooorrrrrrlllllllddddddd, " he shouted at the cameras and the Tillises. "Ain't I pretty."

Sportswriters and newsmen swarmed around that man, my new idol, who puffed around the ring like a peacock showin off his stuff. Microphones and bright camera lights shoved through the smoke to get close to Clay. "Eat your words!" he screamed in their faces, all the time smilin to himself as he played with them. "Ain't I pretty!"

No one in that small, dark living room on Virgin Street knew what was goin on in my little black head that famous night when Cassius Clay beat Sonny Liston, but I knew I knew God was talkin to me through that man. God gave me a message that night I still remember. *"You* will *be a boxer*—you *will be in the ring of champions."* I was thinkin big now.

~

Excerpted from: Thinkin' Big, James "Quick" Tillis as told to J. Engleman Price, published by ECW Press Ltd., 2000, 9781550224306

[FOUR]

Clay vs. Liston I

By Newsweek Staff

Cassius Clay's defeat of Sunny Liston shocked the boxing world. Before taking up boxing, Liston led a gang of thugs who committed muggings and armed robberies on the streets of St. Louis. It was in jail that he first took up boxing. Liston became the world heavyweight champion in 1962 when he knocked out Floyd Paterson in the first round. In the following excerpt, Newsweek looked back at its coverage from the 1964 Clay-Liston fight. —K.M.

Muhammad Ali has died at the age of 74. Newsweek profiled the beloved boxer in 1964, on the occasion of his historic heavyweight championship upset. "My name is magic," declared the 22-year-old athlete, who was still going by his given name, Cassius Marcellus Clay. This story originally appeared in the March 9, 1964 issue of our magazine, with the headline "And I'm Already the Greatest!"

They carried the corned beef out of the ballroom. They cased up the gin, wheeled away the canopied bar, and turned out the lights. Sonny Liston's victory party at the grand and gaudy Fontainebleau Hotel in Miami Beach was over before it began.

Incredibly, the man believed to be the most powerful athlete of his time had given up the sports world's most valuable title while sitting, quietly glowering and in full possession of his senses, on the ring stool. Outlandishly, 22-year-old Cassius Marcellus Clay had become world heavyweight champion.

And it seemed wrong—on so many counts. Some doubted that Liston, who had been throwing lefts all night, had injured his left upper arm badly enough to quit. Others—and they weren't all plump sportswriters—recalled doughtier champions: John L. Sullivan spitting out teeth and then wading into Jake Kilrain; Sugar Ray Robinson fighting himself into heat prostration against Joey Maxim; broken-knuckled Gene Fullmer battling on against Florentino Fernandez. Still others simply could not believe in any upset by an 8-to-1 underdog, even given the reputation of the fight game and Liston's own criminal record and underworld associations.

Menace:

Finally, the fight seemed wrong because the new champion was so anticlimactic. Liston had been the epitome of power and menace. With a glower, a thick-armed gesture, he transfixed before he punished. But Cassius Clay was immaturity itself, a brash, over-handsome movie actor of a fighter.

At times he was hysterical. "I'm the greatest—the prettiest that ever was!" he had screamed at the weigh-in, and the reporters had stared with something of the horror of the normal for the possessed. Sonny Liston, weighing 218 to Clay's 210½ and watching with contempt, made a circular motion with his hand over his forehead. For his wild antics, Clay was fined $2,500 by the Miami Beach Boxing Commission. The commission doctor said the young challenger was "scared to death." So strikingly odd was his behavior that later reporters waited at his dressing-room door to see if he would actually emerge.

Smooth:

He did. He walked past the reporters as if he were any other fighter before a match, and later he went into the ring like any other fighter. And he went to work like no other fighter Liston has faced since Eddie Machen lasted 12 rounds with him almost four years ago. Before a half-empty auditorium (8,297 spectators; the promoters lost $400,000 on the house), and more than 600,000 watching via 371 Theater Network Television hookups (they paid more than $3.5 million), he moved smoothly and swiftly around the thick, lumbering Liston. Sonny threw punch after punch, trying for a quick knockout, wrenching his left upper arm at this time, so he said later. But Clay stayed away, his arms mockingly low, countering now and then, not running, but not trying to slug back either. ("If Patterson had done that, he'd still be champion," Cus D'Amato, the ex-champ's adviser, grumbled.)

Clay won the first round; Liston, the aggressor, took the second, but it was slow going, and Clay was still fighting his own fight. In the third Clay opened a cut under Liston's eye which later needed six stitches. In the fourth round Liston seemed to connect solidly, but Clay never wavered and now he was bruising other parts of Liston's face. "I never seen him cut before," said heavyweight Marty Marshall, who until last week was the only man to defeat Sonny.

Clay came back to his corner after Round 4, looking nimble and still unmarked, but he rolled his head suddenly in pain and clutched his eyes. "I can't see," he gasped to his trainer, Angelo Dundee. "Cut off my gloves. Call off the fight." Frantically Dundee worked over the eyes, trying to discover what had gotten into them. (He never did.) Finally he pushed the fighter to his feet. "This is the big one, Daddy," he said. "Let's not louse it up."

Now came Clay's finest moments. Nearly blind, he staved off

Liston's heavy rushes, avoided blow after blow. Sensing a new weakness in his opponent, the old champion put on the pressure. But it wasn't enough. Again he could not stagger Clay; indeed, he looked amateurish in his attempts. Repeatedly Cassius snaked out a long left hand and seemed to rest it on Liston's bulbous nose as he kept the champion out of range. "I could have broken that arm for him," Liston said later.

Countdown:

Clay's vision cleared toward the end of the round and referee Barney Felix, who later said he had been about to award a TKO to Liston, changed his mind and let the fight continue. In Round 6 Clay was moving cleanly and swiftly again. The round ended and to most observers the fight was about even on points at this time. But Clay was fresh and vibrant, on his feet at the ten-second buzzer. Liston, still seated, looked old, with middle-age folds of neck flesh behind his head over the hugely muscled shoulders. And Liston still sat. Clay moved his lips, counting as is his habit after the warning buzzer, "1–2–3–4–5–6–7 . . . "

Suddenly he pranced about, raised his arms in victory, and gave a delighted whoop. "I'm the greatest," he yelled. "King . . . I'm king!"

He had seen Liston spit out his mouthpiece, had known before the crowd that the champion had quit.

Half an hour later he had a fast, unorganized press conference; indeed, it was more a press confrontation. "Who's the greatest?" he crowed at the bewildered writers who had overwhelmingly discounted his chances. "Who's the greatest?" A few answered half-heartedly. Unsatisfied, he kept haranguing them, kept asking the question. Finally a few more appeased him with a "Cassius Clay." Then, though no one had asked the question, he shouted: "You can't call it a fix. I didn't stop the fight."

Next day Cassius was a new man—or a new boy. He faced the reporters again and spoke slowly and with dignity. But if the message was lower keyed, it was as garbled as ever. In a single five-minute period he promised Liston a rematch, offered to fight anybody, "even two contenders at once," and then said he might retire because he didn't like fighting and hurting people. Unsmiling, he warmed to his favorite topic. "Everybody loves me now. My name is magic. I'm a wise man, not dumb. A dumb man couldn't think up a $7 million gate."

Muslim:

Later he was asked if he was a Black Muslim. "I believe in Islam," he said. "I'm not a Christian. But why's everybody so shook up when I say that? I don't wanta marry no white woman, don't wanta break down no school doors where I'm not wanted."

Liston came to his own press conference in black glasses, a blue arm sling, and a small cheek patch. Never had he seemed so relaxed, so approachable. As the fight wore on, he said, his left glove felt "like it was full of water." He belittled Clay, saying several men he'd beaten were better fighters. "Patterson came to win or lose," Liston said. "He didn't run or hide like he stole somethin'." Asked why he showed so little emotion over losing the title, Liston answered enigmatically, "We can only sing together. We can't talk together." Closing the conference, someone called out "Thank you, Mr. President," the way White House press conferences are closed. There followed a scattering of applause, and Liston looked surprised, then pleased and touched.

By now certain new details were coming out. Eight doctors had examined Liston and certified that the tendon of his left bicep had in truth been torn and divided, that he probably couldn't have properly defended himself. The boxing commission, which had threatened to impound Liston's purse, changed its mind. Soon after, the Internal Revenue Service filed liens against it for tax purposes. And when it came out that a day before the match Liston's company, Inter-continental Promotions, Inc., had paid $50,000 for the right to promote Clay's next fight if he won the championship and to name his opponent, Sen. Philip Hart, Michigan Democrat, threatened a

Congressional investigation. Meanwhile, betting centers all over the country had been checked, and nowhere had the odds fluctuated as they normally do when a fix is in. (But rumors persisted New York odds on the fight had suddenly dropped to 4½–1.)

In His Corner:

If Liston's claim is accepted that his upper arm was hurt early in the fight, his subsequent awkwardness and inability to hurt Clay were explained. Liston is primarily a left-hand puncher, but his power and timing were gone—he couldn't twist his arm properly as he landed—and he badly needed his left to fight a running opponent. The fact that he chose to lose in his corner rather than allow himself to be chopped to bits during nine more rounds proved only that, beneath the sullen animal gaze and under the frightening body, there is a sensible, civilized man. In defeat, Liston seemed as never before to have entered the human race.

To the press the fight was an unmitigated embarrassment. Columnist Jerry Izenberg of the Newhouse newspapers hurried a note to his sports desk. "Please burn, kill and otherwise destroy early column. It could have been worse. I could have picked the Japs in WW II." In a poll of sportswriters on hand, 46 had said Liston would win, and only three had voted for Clay. But even writers from other fields had jumped on the noisy youngster's back. Hearst columnist Frank Conniff predicted "a fistic travesty." Norman Mailer, covering for *Esquire* and sitting next to Gloria Guinness of *Harper's Bazaar* and Truman Capote, recalled the weigh-in and said, "He's close to dementia now." After the fight the *Herald Tribune*'s Red Smith was ruefully eating his own prose: "The words don't taste so good, but they taste better than they read." And chirpy Arthur Daley of *The New York Times* was gamely searching for nice things to say about Clay, after columns of denigration.

Money:

And what of Cassius himself . . . ? Ahead loomed Selective Service, and with his religious beliefs, Cassius might well claim to be a conscientious objector. Alternatively, there was the rematch possibility, with doctors saying Liston could begin training in three months. Ahead also was a very great deal of money, and the first glum Madison Avenue reaction ("He wouldn't be believable endorsing products") was fast reversing. Offers were pouring in. Three days after the fight a rhythm-and-blues record he had cut last fall suddenly took off; more than 100,000 requests for it were made in one day.

But Cassius Clay is young and his world lies ahead. In its own way the heavyweight championship, like the Presidency, is a great uplifter. It made a man of poise and affluence out of Rocky Marciano, a civic leader of Floyd Patterson, and it even seemed to humanize Sonny Liston. Cassius may grow, he may change. "Only 22 years old and I'm already the greatest!" he exulted in the first moments of victory. And he is a young 22, if not younger than springtime, at least as young as the youngest Beatle. There is no limit to his horizon.

~

"Muhammad Ali in 1964: 22 and Already the Greatest," June 7, 2016, originally published March 9, 1964. Licensed from Newsweek.

[FIVE]

Ali and the Nation of Islam

By Mike Marqusee

Muhammad Ali joined the Nation of Islam in 1962. At the time, Mike Marqusee writes, it was the largest, richest black nationalist organization in the country. The organization taught clean living and black pride and published a popular newspaper called Muhammad Speaks. But its teachings were not confined to the Koran. Founder Elijah Muhammad taught that a black scientist named Yacub created the white race more than six thousand years ago to be a race of devils. In the following excerpt, Marqusee explores Ali's relationship with the NOI and Malcom X. Marqusee, an American journalist and political activist, died in 2015. —K.M.

~

In September 1963, the *Philadelphia Daily News* reported that Cassius Clay had attended a Nation of Islam rally in the city. Clay told reporters he was not a Muslim, and the media seemed happy to write off the incident as another one of Cassius's bizarre stunts.

On 5 November, the deal for the Liston fight was signed. For Malcolm, this was an obvious opportunity for the Nation, but Elijah urged Malcolm to keep his distance from the new challenger. He believed Clay would lose to Liston and that the Nation would be diminished by its association with him, a belief which betrayed his own creeping cynicism and lack of imagination. Unlike the rest of the black press, *Muhammad Speaks* failed to report the build-up to the fight and sent no reporters to cover it.

Malcolm did not keep his distance from Clay, nor did he respect a weightier injunction which issued from Chicago in the hours following the Kennedy assassination on 22 November. Elijah had decided that there was no milage to be had in bucking the tide of national grief. Accordingly, he ordered his ministers to refrain from any critical comments about the president whom they had routinely denounced as a "devil" for three years. In New York City on 1 December, in answer to questions from the press, Malcolm reminded Americans that the Kennedy administration had practiced political violence in Africa and Asia, and had sanctioned the assassinations of Lumumba in the Congo and Diem in Vietnam. The killing of JFK was, he said, a case of "chickens coming home to roost . . . . Being an old farm boy myself, chickens coming home to roost never did make me sad. They've always made me glad."

Press and politicians reacted to Malcolm's shock tactics with outrage. More significantly, so did Elijah Muhammad, who summoned Malcolm to Chicago to tell him, without a trace of irony, that "the president of the country is our president too." Malcolm's statement, Elijah said, was a major blunder for which his fellow Muslims would pay dearly. It was imperative that the Nation distance itself from his ill-judged comments, and therefore he would be suspended for ninety days, during which time he was not to make any public statements. Muhammad Speaks eulogized the slain president and gave prominence to the Messenger's decision to discipline his most famous apostle.

Elijah's response to the JFK assassination reflected both short- and long-term considerations. Bitter experience had taught him to fear the power of the federal government and the ire of the media. In particular, he wished to avoid another House Un-American Activities Committee investigation, not least because of the scrutiny his business empire would come under. His fear of repression was matched by his fear of schism. In the coming weeks, Elijah would come to see Malcolm X as the biggest threat to his carefully husbanded authority, his status in the movement and his personal wealth. He proceeded step by step to isolate Malcolm, undercutting his base in the organization, testing the loyalties of the membership.

The first death threat reached Malcolm's ears in late December. In his autobiography, he says that learning of Elijah Muhammad's order to eliminate him "was how, finally, I began to arrive at my psychological divorce from the Nation of Islam." In the first week of January 1964, Muhammad replaced Malcolm as minister at the Harlem mosque, and at their last private meeting he accused his disciple of plotting against him. Meanwhile, Muslim ministers whom Malcolm had trained were denouncing the Messenger's former favorite in mosques across the country.

On 15 January, under increasing pressure from both the Nation of Islam and the FBI, who dogged his every step, Malcolm phoned Clay in Miami, where he was training for the Liston fight, and told him he wanted to take up his offer to visit the challenger's camp with his family. According to the FBI report of the monitored phone call, Clay said, "That's the best news I've heard all day!" and offered to pick up Malcolm and his family at the airport. The next day Clay, Osman Karriem and Clarence X Gill, a Muslim bodyguard, met Malcolm's party and, with an FBI tail in tow, drove them to the black hotel where the challenger's entourage was staying.

Clay told reporters he had given Malcolm and his wife Betty the round-trip all-expenses-paid vacation as a present for their sixth wedding anniversary. Later, Malcolm's daughters were to recall the Miami escapade as a rare interlude of family togetherness in the hectic and highly public life of their father. The day after their arrival, they helped Cassius celebrate his twenty-second birthday. Two days later Betty and the children flew back to New York, but

Malcolm remained. Clay must have been aware that Malcolm was under suspension, that he had been barred from talking to the press and that the Messenger would frown on any association with him. Yet he kept Malcolm in his camp and made no secret of it.

On 21 January, Clay interrupted his training routine to fly to New York with Malcolm. There he addressed a rally at Rockland Palace, where Robeson had once breathed defiance to the white world. (Only a month before, Robeson had returned to the United States after six years abroad, ill and depressed, and promptly retreated into seclusion.) Malcolm helped Clay prepare his speech, but because he was under suspension, he was not allowed to attend the rally. Clay delivered a twenty-minute address to the 1600 Muslims packed into the hall. He asked for their support in his fight against Liston and read them some poetry. "I'm training on lamb chops and that big ugly bear is training on pork chops," he declared to loud applause. He also mentioned Malcolm X, perhaps the last time anyone was to say anything pleasant about the one-time national minister from an official Nation of Islam platform. Clay insisted he was "proud to walk the streets of Miami with Malcolm X." He noted, as he often did in the coming years, that Muslims refrained from smoking and drinking. "This is a miracle for the so-called Negroes, and this is why the white man is all shook up." An FBI informant was in the hall, noted Clay's presence and rushed outside to tip off the local media. Clay's apparent link to the Nation of Islam, a story which had been gestating for several months, was now out in the open and made front-page news the next day. In a revealing formulation, Clay was repeatedly asked by the press whether he was "a card-carrying member of the Black Muslims." "Card-carrying; what's does that mean?" he answered. "I'm a race man and every time I go to a Muslim meeting I get inspired." In a banner headline, the *Amsterdam News* reported the story, "Cassius Clay Almost Says He's a Muslim." The front pages of the black press were splashed with photos of the young fighter playing with Malcolm X's family. Elijah Muhammad must have been beside himself. The press hardly noticed when Clay took his military qualifying examination on 24 January. His results were so poor—he placed in the sixteenth percentile, way below the qualifying standard—that they roused suspicion, and Clay was asked to re-take the test after the Liston fight.

George Plimpton, who was to spend more than a decade covering Ali's career, was perplexed by Clay's connection with the Muslims and sought out Malcolm for an interview. Despite Elijah's proscription, Malcolm met Plimpton at the Hampton House Hotel in the heart of black Miami. A deep discomfort runs through the published version of the encounter, which appeared in Harper's in June 1964. "He often smiles broadly," Plimpton noted, "but not with humor." Behind the articulate exterior, Plimpton descried a "truly intractable" character. But, as the writer faithfully records this "intractable," "caustic" man was also the first to detect the seriousness underlying Cassius Clay's antics, and to see in the loudmouth underdog the lineaments of the future Muhammad Ali. "Not many people know the quality of the mind he's got in there," Malcolm explained. "He fools them. One forgets that though a clown never imitates a wise man, the wise man can imitate the clown. He is sensitive, very humble, yet shrewd—with as much untapped mental energy as he has physical power." Noting that "our religion removes fear," he predicted Clay would topple Liston, then added, "We believe in exercise, physical fitness, but as for commercial sport, that's a racket. Commercial sport is the pleasure of the idle rich. The vice of gambling stems from it . . . . The Negro never comes out ahead—never one in the history of sport."

Malcolm liked to speak of himself as Clay's "older brother," a political mentor and spiritual guide. According to Malcolm's wife, Betty Shabazz, he spent hours talking with Cassius about the meaning of the title fight and the fighter's destiny in his people's future. As always, Malcolm's aim was to clear his disciple's mind of the disabling preconceptions bred by a racist society, to inculcate self-confidence through a deep, guiding sense of purpose. Like Frantz Fanon and C.L.R. James, Malcolm had studied the psychology of the oppressed, and much of his teaching was aimed at overcoming the psychological advantages that the rich and powerful always enjoy over the poor and weak. He believed that freedom demanded nothing less than a radical recreation of the self. What he was doing with Clay was what he had been doing in the Nation and what he was to continue to do in the last year of his life: preparing the actors of history for their role in it.

But for Malcolm himself, these days in Miami passed in a haze of anxiety and growing despair. "Whatever I was saying at any time was being handled by a small corner of my mind. The rest of my mind was filled with a parade of a thousand and one different scenes from the past," he reported to Alex Haley. "I told the various sportswriters repeatedly what I gradually had come to know within myself was a lie—that I would be reinstated within ninety days." Despite Malcolm's claims of reticence, it seems unlikely that he never discussed his worries with his host, the man with whom he was sharing the media spotlight. The depiction of Clay in these months as an innocent, unaware or unaffected by the struggle between Malcolm and Muhammad, is not credible. He was providing shelter and publicity to, and spending hours in private conversation with, a Muslim known to be at odds with the Messenger.

In early February Clay told the *Louisville Courier-Journal*, "I like the Muslims. I'm not going to get killed trying to force myself on people who don't want me. I like my life. Integration is wrong. The white people don't want integration. I don't believe in forcing it, and the Muslims don't believe in it. So what's wrong with the Muslims?" According to the paper, Clay's father, Cassius Sr., said both his sons had joined the organization, and accused the Nation of "ruining" his boys. As rumors circulated, panic gripped the fight promoters. Ticket sales had been slow, and it was feared that the challenger's association with the Muslims could generate a backlash against the fight. Clay was quick to spot the potential for a role reversal and told Liston: "I make you great. The fans love you because I'm the villain." Clay may have been amused, but his publicist, Harold Conrad, despaired: "The whole sales pitch for the fight had been Clay against Liston, white hat against black hat, and now it looked like there'd be two black hats fighting."

It was a measure of Malcolm's symbolic power in the mind of white America that his mere presence by the side of the challenger could transform the values hitherto attached to the contest, and threaten its future. For Cassius Clay, this was a moment of truth, the first of many which he was to face in the coming years. It was made clear to him by friends, managers, promoters and journalists that it would be in his interest to renounce the Muslims. They told him he would be crazy to let this association jeopardize the chance of a lifetime, a chance he himself had worked so hard to secure. Quietly but firmly, the young fighter stood his ground. A compromise was agreed: there would be no statement, but Malcolm X would leave the camp, at least for the time being.

Meanwhile, the FBI was circulating details of the rift between Malcolm and Muhammad, reports of which began to appear in the mainstream press. Malcolm returned to Miami on 23 February, and was once again met by Clay at the airport, accompanied by Osman Karriem and Clarence X Gill. According to the FBI, Clay asked, "Any word from Chicago?" and Malcolm replied, "Nothing positive." Later, when the two men were approached by a *Miami Herald* reporter, Malcolm would make only one comment, "If you think Cassius Clay was loud, wait until I start talking on the first of March."

On the morning of the fight, 25 February, Malcolm phoned Elijah Muhammad. Muhammad accused Malcolm of attempting to blackmail him; Malcolm denied the charge. That night, in the dressing room before the fight, Malcolm prayed with Cassius and his brother Rudolph (later Rahaman Ali). Unlike almost everyone else, including Elijah Muhammad, Malcolm X had always believed that Clay could win the fight. "It was Allah's intent for me to help Cassius prove Islam's superiority before the world—through proving that mind can win over brawn." He fortified Clay to face Liston by retelling the tale of David and Goliath. For Malcolm, Liston's whole life and career were proof that the struggle for integration was futile and debilitating. Clay, he felt, could represent something different. "Clay . . . is the finest Negro athlete I have ever known, the man who will mean more to his people than Jackie Robinson, because

Robinson is the white man's hero." Malcolm saw Clay's symbolic power more clearly than anyone else at the time, and he helped Clay to realize that power in the ring:

> *"This fight is the truth," I told Cassius. "It's the Cross and the Crescent fighting in a prize ring—for the first time. It's a modern crusades—a Christian and a Muslim facing each other with television to beam it off Telstar for the whole world to see what happens!" I told Cassius, "Do you think Allah has brought about all this, intending for you to leave the ring as anything but the champion?"*

Malcolm sat prominently at the ringside, where he chatted to Clay's other star guest, Sam Cooke. Live attendance was disappointing but over one million people watched the fight on closed-circuit TV. A somewhat mystified *New York Times reporter* described the atmosphere at the screening in Harlem: "The general support for Clay seemed to transcend any betting considerations and even the normal empathy for an underdog."

In Miami, Clay danced his way around a lumbering Liston, his speed, footwork and amazing 360-degree ring-vision nullifying the champion's advantages in power and reach. When a bewildered and dejected Liston failed to come out for the seventh round, Clay was jubilant. "I want everyone to bear witness," he shouted. "I am the greatest! I shook up the world!" Many sportswriters, however, regarded the upset victory as a fluke. Malcolm was more perceptive: "The secret of one of fight history's greatest upsets was that, months before that night, Clay had out-thought Liston." Because of his rejection of the prevailing stereotypes of black sportsmen, Malcolm was able to see in Clay what the sportswriters refused to see: a supremely intelligent and inventive boxer inspired by more than just a lust for money. That night Clay received a telegram from Martin Luther King, the only black leader, besides Malcolm, to congratulate him on his victory.

Back in the Hampton House Hotel, in the euphoric hours after the fight, Malcolm phoned Alex Haley to share the good news. Haley recalled Malcolm's childlike delight that the new heavyweight champion was sitting next door. Perhaps at this juncture he entertained a flickering belief that this spectacular turn of events would sway the balance in his struggle with Elijah Muhammad. But even as Malcolm exulted on the telephone, Clay was telling Jim Brown that he would have to break with Malcolm and follow Elijah. Judging by his behavior in the next few days, however, Clay's mind was not entirely made up, and he may have hoped for some reconciliation between the two leaders.

On the day after Clay's public embrace of the Nation of Islam, both the FBI and the Department of Defense began inquiries into the new champion's Selective Service status. At a press conference, the Louisville draft board chairman said he expected Clay to be called up "within weeks." No one paid much attention because of the furore surrounding Clay's conversion to the Nation, which at that time seemed more likely to scupper his boxing career than the US military.

For the first time in a decade, Malcolm X was absent from the annual Savior's Day rally, held that evening in Chicago. In Malcolm's place, warming up the crowd for the Messenger, was Louis X of Boston. In front of an ecstatic crowd of five thousand, Muhammad confirmed to the world that Cassius Clay was his follower and claimed credit, with Allah, for his great victory. "I'm so glad that Cassius Clay was brave enough to say that he was a Muslim. . . He was able, by confessing that Allah was his god and by following Muhammad, to whip a much tougher man. They wanted him to get his face torn up, but Allah and myself said 'No!' . . . Clay has confidence in Allah, and in me as his only messenger." Through his brother Rudolph, who had flown up from Miami, Clay sent a message to the faithful, thanking them for their prayers.

~

[SIX]

Ali vs. Chuvalo I

By George Chuvalo with Murray Greig

Even before he was officially banned from boxing, Ali's position on the war in Vietnam made it increasingly difficult to find U.S. cities willing to host his fights. Despite pressure from veterans' groups, Toronto stepped in to host Ali's last-minute bout against George Chuvalo, whose career record was 34–11–2. —K.M.

I was sitting in Ungerman's office on the afternoon of March 12, 1966, when the telephone rang. Irving picked it up and told the caller I was there with him, so he put it on the speaker. "Hi, George . . . this is Mike Malitz in New York. I'll get right to the point: How'd you like to fight Ali for the title on March 29?"

Malitz was executive vice-president of Main Bout Inc., a group of investors that also included Ali's manager, Herbert Muhammad; lawyer Bob Arum (this fight marked his first foray into boxing); Nation of Islam national secretary John Ali; and Jim Brown, the great NFL running back who retired after the 1965 season. Their plan for a title showdown with Ernie Terrell had fallen apart, so they were looking for somebody to take Terrell's place.

It was only 17 days' notice, but Malitz knew I'd take it if we were fighting in 17 minutes. Still, I decided to have a little fun. "Sounds pretty good, Mike . . . but I gotta talk to my wife first and see if we're doing anything on the 29th. I'll call you right back."

Then I called Lynne.

"Lynne, what are we doing on the 29th of this month?" I asked.

"Nothing, why?"

"'Cause you're going to the fights."

"Who's fighting?"

"Me"

"Who are you fighting?"

"Muhammad Ali."

My wife started laughing.

"No, doll. For real."

I went back on the other line. "Hey, Mike, it's okay. I'm free." Actually, I wasn't. A couple of weeks earlier, we'd signed a contract with promoter Chris Dundee to fight Levi Forte on March 29 in Miami. Once the bout with Ali was announced, Dundee threatened to get a court injunction to stop it. It was all for show, because Chris wasn't about to screw his brother Angie out of a payday with Ali, but Ungerman ended up piecing him off anyway. On top of that, there had been a press conference just a couple of days earlier, confirming that it would be Ali and Terrell at Maple Leaf Gardens on the 29th, so this really was an 11th-hour deal.

Malitz's offer wasn't much—20 per cent of the gate, plus a piece of the theater TV sales—but to my way of thinking it was a now-or-never proposition and I didn't want to blow the opportunity. It was a rush job, like having five minutes to get ready for a date with a beautiful woman (like Raquel Welch!) You've got to get shaved and showered, brush your teeth, comb your hair. There's no time to prepare the way you really should.

That's what it felt like when I got the offer, but I knew I had to go for it. Plus, I fully expected to win. I figured once I had the title, the money would follow.

Main Bout's plan for an Ali-Terrell showdown had started to fall apart almost from the moment they announced it.

The fight was originally scheduled to take place in Rutherford, New Jersey, but there was so much heat from war veterans over Ali's anti-Vietnam stance that the plug was pulled almost immediately. The New York State Athletic Commission also refused to license it because of Terrell's connections to Glickman and his cronies, so Main Bout then tried Philadelphia, which slammed the door. Even Muhammad's hometown of Louisville said no after the Kentucky state senate passed a resolution that read, "His attitude brings discredit to all loyal Kentuckians and to the names of the thousands who gave their lives for this country during his lifetime." The next attempt was Chicago, but the Illinois Athletic Commission didn't want the fight, either.

Main Bout then looked north and contacted promoter Loren Cassina, who tried to put together a deal for the fight to take place in Montreal. Cassina got Mayor Jean Drapeau on board, but then the American Legion contacted Drapeau and told him that if the fight took place, they would organize a boycott of Expo 67. Drapeau quickly backed down.

The reception was the same in Verdun, Quebec. Offers came in from Vancouver, Edmonton and two Ontario cities Kingston and tiny Cobourg—before Main Bout finally settled on Toronto.

For a time everything seemed set for the fight to take place at Maple Leaf Gardens, but then Terrell's manager of record, Bernie Glickman, made a near-fatal miscalculation.

No doubt recalling how easy it was to scare the shit out of Ungerman prior to my fight with Ernie four months earlier, Glickman went to see Herbert Muhammad, who besides being Ali's manager and promoter was the No. 2 man in the Nation of Islam. Glickman must have posed the same threat that he used on Ungerman . . . just a different lake: if Ali won the fight, Herbert would end up in a cement box at the bottom of Lake Michigan.

But Glickman wasn't dealing with the likes of Ungerman this time. All Herbert had to do was snap his fingers and a couple of his Black Muslim henchmen, better known as the Fruit of Islam, would pound Glickman to a pulp. He was interrogated by the police but he wouldn't talk. He went directly from the hospital to a mental institution and never saw the light of day again. The next day, Terrell announced he was pulling out.

That's how I ended up getting my first fight with Ali.

Terrell claimed he pulled out because Main Bout backed down on his guarantee—supposedly $50,000 from the live gate and $100,000 from theater TV, plus training expenses—but I think that's total B.S. Glickman's beating sent a very clear signal that nobody, not even the mob, was going to mess with the Nation of Islam.

Even before we made the deal with Malitz, Conn Smythe, the war hero who built Maple Leaf Gardens in 1931, read about plans for the fight while he was vacationing in Florida. Although he'd recently relinquished control of the arena, Smythe retained 5,100 shares in Maple Leaf Gardens Ltd. and a seat on its board of directors.

Ali was the antithesis of everything Smythe stood for, and when he got the news that Toronto was opening its arms to welcome a draft resister who was being so vocal in condemning the Vietnam War, it was more than Smythe could stomach. He called Harold Ballard to confirm the report, then followed up with a letter to the effect that he would resign his directorship and demand that his shares be bought out unless Ballard could guarantee that "Clay" would not be fighting in Maple Leaf Gardens.

The cantankerous Ballard, who wanted the fight all along, had no qualms about accepting Smythe's resignation. Harold promptly cut a deal with Main Bout for a share of the closed-circuit TV rights and told the press he wasn't at all worried about negative publicity.

The same day the TV deal was announced, former light heavyweight champ Billy Conn was interviewed by *The New York Times* and said, "I'll never go to another one of Clay's fights. He is a disgrace to the boxing profession, and I think any American who pays to watch him after what he has said about Vietnam should be ashamed. They should stay away from those closed-circuit television shows."

The Ontario Athletic Commission and some mealy-mouthed Canadian politicians felt the same way. The OAC was under the jurisdiction of the Ontario Department of Labour. The commission's chairman, Merv McKenzie, spinelessly announced he had to consult with Labor Minister Les Rowntree before giving final approval to the fight. McKenzie said he wanted it to be either 14 or 16 rounds so that it couldn't be considered a title bout. With typical Canadian reticence, he told the *Toronto Star*, "I want to clear up whatever political overtones the government might be sensitive to concerning Clay."

Those "overtones" came from the likes of George Ben, a Liberal member of the Ontario Legislature, who grabbed some ink by arguing the fight "would lower the international prestige of Toronto." The Royal Canadian Legion then got in on the act.

In a show of solidarity with its American counterpart, the Legion launched a campaign to pressure theater TV outlets against showing the fight. The political pressure and Legion protests on both sides of the border resulted in nearly 100 of 280 signed outlets canceling the telecast.

In the end, McKenzie and his cohorts decreed that as far as Ontario was concerned, Ali vs. Chuvalo would not be a world championship fight. Instead, they called it a "heavyweight showdown" and ordered that the tickets and souvenir programs bill it as such. There was no concern about posters, because the fight was made on such short notice that none were printed.

The OAC's gutless move really cheapened it for me, making it sound like it was an exhibition. It was so bloody Canadian . . . and it hurt that it was my own province and city that were screwing me. I felt like Gary Cooper in High Noon, being left to face the bad guys all alone. It still angers me today when I see that program, with the caption under Ali's picture that says, "The People's Champion." Virtually everywhere else on the planet he was recognized as the one and only true world champion—but not in good old Ontario.

What was really galling was that these guys were basically just writing me off, like there was no way in the world I could win the fight. And if I did win, my own hometown wouldn't recognize me as the world champion. Thanks for the support!

With few exceptions, the Canadian media lapped up everything that was spoon-fed to them by McKenzie, and none of the Toronto writers had the balls to write how absurd it was to deny that we were having a legitimate world title fight. A columnist in Winnipeg wrote, "If Clay is permitted to have a 'world championship' bout in Toronto, there isn't enough disinfectant in the Dominion to clean the stench out of Maple Leaf Gardens." The headline over Jim Kernaghan's story in the *Toronto Star* was "Clay hated by millions!" In the *Los Angeles Times*, Jim Murray wrote that Ali was "a Black Benedict Arnold" and advised him to never go anywhere near the Lincoln Memorial in Washington "because those will be real tears running down Abe's cheeks."

One of the few writers who showed any guts was *The Ring*'s Nat Fleischer. He really ripped into McKenzie for letting the WBA dictate Ontario's affairs, telling the Canadian Press, "I'm probably setting myself up to be blasted by Mr. McKenzie and his commission, but I've been blasted by far better men."

Personally, I didn't support the Vietnam War either, but I didn't think Ali's stance on it would stir up such a hornet's nest. I didn't talk about his situation, and nobody asked me about it. Maybe it would've been different if I was an American, but all the politics seemed beside the point.

I'd gotten to know Muhammad a little bit ever since our first meeting before I fought Mike DeJohn in 1963, and I liked him—even though he backed out of the deal to fight me after I whipped DeJohn. We'd kibitzed each other with the "Washerwoman" stuff, had fun with it. The poetry, the boasting . . . he got all that from watching Gorgeous George, the wrestler. But Ali took it to another level, and it was refreshing. Boxing had never had a showman like him, and I thought it was great.

But Muhammad was a different guy in the lead-up to our fight;

much more somber and restrained than I'd ever seen him. I remember how quiet and humble he was at the press conference. He told the *Toronto Telegram*, "The people here in Canada are very nice. Honestly, I am not saying that just because I am here. I have never been treated so nice in my whole life. There are no people making wisecracks, everybody is friendly—the children, waiters, hotel people, policemen. Everybody is as nice as they could be. It's a lot different than from where I come from."

You could tell that he felt the sting of being a social pariah in so many ways. Today the man is an icon, the most recognized face on the planet. Everybody loves him now, but it was a much different story in 1966. Back then, a lot of people—white and black—hated him. There were always interviews in the papers and on TV, with people saying, "My kid's in the war, my kid went to Vietnam. What the hell is this guy doing? Who does he think he is?" That kind of thing.

I didn't feel sorry for the guy, but I remember thinking that it must be a hell of a thing when you're despised in your own country and people make it so clear that they don't want you to ever come back home. I thought Muhammad must be a pretty strong guy inside. Here he was, facing the wrath of the U.S. government, the wrath of the army, facing possible imprisonment, facing exile from the fight game and not being able to earn a living in his chosen profession. He was bucking a lot of very powerful people, and for what?

Of course, to the Black Muslims, to millions of black people, Ali was a hero. His courage lifted them up and made them proud. He made them feel good about themselves. I could see how it would be very easy to root for somebody like him, who stood up for what he believed and was willing to accept the consequences. To my way of thinking, Ali was a guy who had some big problems, but I wasn't going to lose any sleep over it. I had enough on my own plate to worry about—and only 17 days to get ready.

In the meantime, Ungerman was in a dither trying to help Teddy and me prepare for the biggest fight of my life. He made sure to let the newspapers know he was "sparing no expense" by bringing Joe

Louis and Rocky Marciano into my camp—again—but it was just window dressing, like it had been for the Terrell fight. Marciano was only interested in getting paid and getting laid, and Joe didn't do much more than pose for pictures.

To be honest, it was a pain in the ass having those guys around. I just wanted to concentrate on training, but Irving was always setting up silly photo ops, with Joe and me sipping tea or Rocky and me looking at film. If that wasn't bad enough, Ungerman also brought in Drew "Bundini" Brown, Ali's longtime cheerleader, confidant and cornerman. They'd had a big falling out a few months earlier over Bundini's refusal to accept the Nation of Islam's ban on drinking, and he was finally kicked out of Ali's entourage after he hocked Muhammad's championship belt to a Harlem barber for $500.

Ungerman wanted Bundini in my corner because he thought it would do a psych job on Ali, but I didn't want to have anything to do with the guy. If Bundini was capable of selling out Ali after everything Muhammad had done for him, what the hell would he try with me? A few days before the fight I told Irving, "Get him the hell out of here. It's like having a spy in my camp!" Bundini didn't stick around after that.

My plan for the fight was simple: as the shorter guy, I wanted to stay close to Ali, nullify his speed and prevent him from using the whole ring. I knew I could hurt him to the body, so I wanted to wear him down and immobilize him to the point where I could knock him out.

I wanted to take him past the 12th round, which would be virgin territory for him. I'd gone 15 rounds with Terrell, but Muhammad had never been there before. I also wanted to make it rough. The rougher, the better. There's more body contact at close quarters, and fights have a different feel at that range. When I'm in close, I feel like I'm the boss and I can impose my will on anybody.

It was a good plan, but the mistake we made, which I never realized at the time, was doing all my sparring in the small ring at the Lansdowne gym, which was like a snake pit.

The two quickest guys I worked with—Billy Joiner and

Alvin "Blue" Lewis—were both fast, slick guys, but I had no trouble at all trapping them on the ropes and banging them to the body. It's okay for a stick-and-move guy to work in a small ring, but for me it was too easy. Lewis, who was still an amateur, went home to Detroit after I busted him up pretty badly in the rib cage. Joiner, the 1962 U.S. Golden Gloves champion at light heavyweight, was 86–6 as an amateur—and two of those losses were to Ali. His style was pretty similar to Muhammad's, and I was handling him with no problem.

Because time was so short, I did more running for this fight than was normal for me. To help with conditioning, we also brought in the renowned fitness guru Lloyd Percival—the guy who wrote the tips on those Kellogg's trading cards I'd studied as a kid. I didn't want Lynne and the boys being bothered by all the distractions, so I moved out of the house and into the Seaway Towers hotel, where I got up at seven in the morning and did four miles of jogging and wind sprints. In the afternoons, Teddy and I went to Lansdowne to spar with Lewis, Joiner or the other guys we had in camp: Hubert Hilton, Greatest Crawford and Richie Pittman, an old-timer who'd been a sparring partner for Ali, Liston and Patterson.

The day before the fight, the Canadian Press ran an interview with Ali and Dundee in which they called me a dirty fighter. "I know he fights dirty, I've seen it, but if Georgie tries it with me he's going to be in real trouble," Ali told the reporter. "Still, I can't figure on putting him away early. He's never been down, let alone out. I had a dream about it. I kept hitting him and hitting him and he wouldn't go down, and pretty soon I was so tired, I could hardly keep punching. He kept punching and getting stronger. Man, I woke up in a sweat."

Dundee was more succinct. "Chuvalo is dirty—and he's good at it," Angelo said. "He's a tough guy who would fight a lion, and he can punch. We gotta watch out for his left. A guy like Chuvalo, you could hit him over the head with a pipe in a dark alley and he would turn around and hurt you with a left hook. We gotta watch out for that."

That Ali was a 7–1 betting favorite struck me as absurd. I remember thinking, "Why should this guy be such an overwhelming favorite to knock me out?" That had never happened before, so why would it happen now? For people to think this was going to be an easy night for Ali seemed to be pretty unsound judgment.

At the official weigh-in, I was 216 pounds and Ali was 214½. On the afternoon of the fight, I had a nice meal of broiled filet of sole and then took a nap. When the bell rang a few hours later, he came directly to me—and it took all of about 30 seconds for me to realize he was the fastest fighter I'd ever seen.

It's one thing to expect it; it's another thing to feel it, live it. When you experience that kind of speed up close, there's nothing to compare it against.

In the opening round, Ali tried to psych me out by holding me close behind the head while exposing his gut, like he was inviting me to rip out his kidneys. I knew what he was doing, holding me close enough so that my punching a short distance wouldn't have that much velocity, but I gladly obliged him by pounding 15 short rights to his ribs. Today, people say to me, "Wow, the cat opened up and let you nail him to the body!" That's true. But if you notice, he only did it once.

For most of the next hour, that was the story. A crowd of 13,540 (which paid what was then a Canadian record gate of about $165,000) watched as I kept trying to bull my way inside while Ali jabbed and moved, relying on his quick feet to get him out of trouble whenever I tried to trap him on the ropes.

Against the ropes is where I wanted him, so I naturally kept going to his body to try to slow him down. Probably 80 per cent of my punches were body shots. Over the years a lot has been said and written about me supposedly deliberately throwing low blows, but that's not true. A few of my punches did land south of the border (one of which was immortalized in a great full-page photo in Life magazine the week after the fight), but in most cases it only looked like they were low because Ali was wearing his cup about six inches higher than normal.

Dundee knew I was a body puncher, so he had a special cup made for Muhammad. It was made to fight George Chuvalo. In order to disguise it, they had to get custom-made trunks. I knew it as soon as I saw Ali in the ring. When I saw the top of his bright red jock a couple of inches above his belt line, I felt like Elmer Fudd when he fought Bugs Bunny. In the cartoon, Bugs wore his trunks up around his ears in order to avoid getting hit.

The referee was a clothing salesman named Jackie Silvers. Like everybody else, he could see that Ali's trunks were way too high, but what could he do about it? Still, I've got to give Silvers credit for letting us fight. He was the complete opposite of what Sammy Luftspring had been when I fought Terrell.

Afterward, in response to Dundee complaining long and loud about my "dirty" tactics, Silvers told the reporters that he "didn't want to ruin a good fight by being too intrusive." I thought that was pretty good. When The Rings Nat Fleischer asked him about it, Silvers replied, "The low punches were of no consequence. They weren't hurting Clay. Chuvalo is not a low-blow hitter, he's a body banger. If you're going to be watching that close for low blows, there would be no fight."

Ali's left hand was like greased lightning, but there wasn't a lot behind it. His jab had more zing than sting, but it was a lot tougher for me to cuff aside, like I did with Terrell. Once in a while he tried to turn the jab into a power punch by putting all his weight behind it, but it wasn't a whole lot harder.

To this day, people say to me, "He really hit you, he really pounded on you." Maybe it looks that way, but I wasn't taking any real hard shots. They weren't nearly as hard as some of the punches I'd taken before, like from Mike DeJohn. And I got hit a lot harder by Mel Turnbow and George Foreman in later fights. But because of Muhammad's speed, because of his movement, a lot of people think I took a real beating. When they ask if I was worried about getting hurt I have to laugh, because in my mind I always said to myself that I couldn't be hurt. In a crazy kind of way, I felt indestructible. If another fighter said that about himself, I'd start laughing, but to my own ego, to my own sense of identity, that's how it was. It made me feel special.

When I say Ali's speed was amazing, I'm not just referring to his hands. When he moved his legs and hands at the same time, when he synchronized them, he was really something. In those days, heavyweights didn't move around very much, so he really looked different. Before him, the only guys I ever saw move around the ring remotely like that were Jersey Joe Walcott and a blown-up light heavyweight, Billy Conn.

What surprised me the most about Muhammad was that he threw so accurately when he was in full motion. He'd be out of punching range, but as he moved back in he would already be starting to throw his punch, right on target. If I waited until he was back in range, it was already too late. I got hit, no question, but I was never hurt and he never landed anything hard in the most dangerous area, which is right along the jawline and up behind the ears. Most of the time he caught me high on the head—and I can take punches high on the head all night long.

As fast as Muhammad was, I still managed to shake him up three or four times. In Rounds 5 and 6 I nailed him with some left hooks that got his attention, and in the 15th I backed him up and had him hurt. He definitely proved he could take a punch—something nobody talked about before our fight, but which everybody wrote about afterward. He had a real talent for riding punches and being able to weather the storm when he was hurt. I know I hurt him to the body at times, and I should have followed up by punching to his head, but he was just too damn quick on his feet.

I'm sometimes still asked why I didn't bob and weave more against Ali instead of going straight forward. The answer is pretty obvious when you watch the film. When you fight a quick guy and try to weave your way inside, you're bent down and not positioned properly to strike, because he's backing up. Bobbing and weaving is only effective when the other guy is right on top of you, but that wasn't where Ali wanted to be with me. At close range I could hurt him—and he knew it.

Under Toronto's five-point must system, Silvers scored the fight 73–63. The two judges, Tony Canzano and Jackie Johnson, had it

74–63. By rounds, Silvers had Ali winning nine and me winning two, with four even. Canzano scored it 12–1–2 and Johnson 13–1–1. *The Ring* scored it 72–62 and gave me Rounds 1, 2 and 12, with Round 8 even.

As the scores were being read, my oldest son, Mitchell, who was six at the time, climbed up into the ring. He gave me a big hug, but he had tears in his eyes. I felt bad for the little guy.

There was a lot of talk about me being the first to go 15 rounds with Ali, and people still bring it up because the fight has been replayed hundreds of times on TV in Canada and the U.S. At first I thought all the talk about my durability was a negative thing, but then I realized it was kind of special. The average person can't conceive what it's like to fight 15 rounds; that was the exclusive property of world champions and top-10 contenders. And now that the championship distance is 12 rounds, it will never happen again, so I guess it was special. And I can't imagine anything that comes close to matching what that feels like.

When people meet me and say, "George, you went the distance with Muhammad Ali!" I say, "No, you've got it wrong. He went the distance with me." When it was all over, he was the guy who went to the hospital because he was pissing blood. Me? I got to go dancing with my wife. No question I got the best of that deal.

In a crazy way, that fight is what defines me for a lot of my fellow Canadians, but it took a long time before I came to appreciate how good it made them feel. It happened almost 50 years ago, but I still hear it all the time, that it made Canadians proud. I feel happy about that, because it means the fight will kind of live forever. A day doesn't go by that I don't get asked about it, and it's always the same: "Hey George, you rumbled with Muhammad Ali! What a great fight!"

Although I was disappointed about losing to Ali, it was nice to finally get some positive press. Not surprisingly, it was mostly from U.S. writers rather than Canadians. Gilbert Rogin's cover story in *Sports Illustrated* was headlined "A Battle of the Lionhearted" and described me as being "far tougher and more persevering than any lion, and it was these attributes which made the fight." The *New York*

Herald Tribune story said, "George Chuvalo deserves an apology from all who derided him. One-sided as a fight could be in points, he made this a memorable battle. It was a far, far better show than anyone could have expected. There wasn't anything questionable or distasteful about it." The *New York Times* report took a similar turn: "Some of us said that this Canadian should have been selling peanuts in the aisles rather than throwing punches in the ring. We were wrong. Cassius Clay has never been given a harder, more bruising fight. Chuvalo was the honest worker. He comes to fight. He wasn't scared, or cocky or overconfident. He was willing to take a lot of punishment for the opportunity to give some. And he did."

Even Joe Louis weighed in. He was signed up by the Canadian Press to write a ringside report, which was published under his byline in papers all across the country. "They can run and most of the time they can hide," wrote Joe. "Cassius Clay hid long enough for George Chuvalo to get tired, so he's still heavyweight champion of the world. But don't let anyone say that George didn't make this the best heavyweight championship fight since Rocky Marciano knocked out Archie Moore in 1956."

Ali told the *Toronto Star* I was the toughest guy he'd fought to that point, adding, "I kept saying he was tough—tougher than Liston, tougher than Patterson—but people thought I was just trying to build up the gate. Now you know I was right." That was nice—as was the last word from Dundee, who told the *Star*, "Chuvalo fought the greatest fight of his life. Canadians ought to be real proud of this man. I was proud of him . . . and I was in the other guy's corner."

As for my minuscule payday, it wasn't until decades later that I learned more, after Globe and Mail sportswriter William Houston got hold of the old accounting books from Maple Leaf Gardens. According to the MLG records, Ali received $125,000 and I was paid $49,000. Off the top, Irving pocketed $24,000 from my cut as a promoter's fee, even though the Ontario Athletic Commission's regulation that prohibited managers from promoting cards on which their fighters appeared. According to the terms of our contract, that left me with 50 per cent of the remaining $25,000—meaning that

I fought 15 grueling rounds with one of the greatest champions in boxing history for $12,500 . . . in Canadian money, no less!

Contrary to his self-proclaimed and carefully cultivated philanthropic image, Ungerman entitled himself to $36,500 from my total purse of $49,000—and for that piece of the action he never had to take a single punch. I can only imagine the kind of creative accounting he came up with for several other of my fights that he promoted.

Oh yeah, one other thing. The night after the fight, Lynne and I, my cousin Eddie and his wife, Millie, were among several hundred Torontonians who reported seeing three UFOs alternately hovering and then moving at high speed across the sky above the city. With colors ranging from a glowing white to red, green and blue, the objects were unlike any commercial aircraft I'd ever seen before—or since.

The authorities never issued an official explanation for the mass sighting, but I like to think that maybe Muhammad and I had some extraterrestrial fight fans tapping into that closed-circuit telecast . . .

~

[SEVEN]

"I Just Wanted to Be Free"

By Muhammad Ali

Considerable scholarship has been focused on the complexities of Muhammad Ali's draft refusal. Was he a hero? A conscientious objector? Being used by the Nation of Islam? Here is Ali's own explanation, written more than three decades after the fact.
—K.M.

~

I never thought of myself as great when I refused to go into the army. All I did was stand up for what I believed. There were people who thought the war in Vietnam was right. And those people, if they went to war, acted just as brave as I did. There were people who tried to put me in jail. Some of them were hypocrites, but others did what they thought was proper and I can't condemn them for following their consciences either. People say I made a sacrifice, risking jail and my whole career. But God told Abraham to kill his son and Abraham was willing to do it, so why shouldn't I follow what

I believed? Standing up for my religion made me happy; it wasn't a sacrifice. When people got drafted and sent to Vietnam and didn't understand what the killing was about and came home with one leg and couldn't get jobs, that was a sacrifice. But I believed in what I was doing, so no matter what the government did to me, it wasn't a loss.

Some people thought I was a hero. Some people said that what I did was wrong. But everything I did was according to my conscience. I wasn't trying to be a leader. I just wanted to be free. And I made a stand all people, not just black people, should have thought about making, because it wasn't just black people being drafted. The government had a system where the rich man's son went to college, and the poor man's son went to war. Then, after the rich man's son got out of college, he did other things to keep him out of the army until he was too old to be drafted. So what I did was for me, but it was the kind of decision everyone has to make. Freedom means being able to follow your religion but it also means carrying the responsibility to choose between right and wrong. So when the time came for me to make up my mind about going into the army, I knew people were dying in Vietnam for nothing and I knew I should live by what I thought was right. I wanted America to be America. And now the whole world knows that, so far as my own beliefs are concerned, I did what was right for me.

~

[EIGHT]

The Exile of Muhammad Ali

By Dahleen Glanton

Dahleen Glanton is a metro reporter for the Chicago Tribune. In this piece, she talks about the life Ali spent in Chicago after he was banned from boxing for refusing the draft. —K.M.

~

During his years exiled from the boxing ring, dethroned heavyweight champion Muhammad Ali found refuge on the South Side of Chicago.

Stripped of his boxing title after refusing to fight in the Vietnam War, Ali immersed himself in Islam, his newfound religion. And as the country that once hailed him as "The Greatest" cast him aside, the South Side—home of the Nation of Islam—stepped in to embrace him.

Shortly after announcing that he had converted to Islam in 1964, Ali spent more than a decade in and out of Chicago. He first settled into a small, third-floor apartment in the 7000 block of South

Cregier Avenue. By the time he left Chicago for good in the late 1970s, he had bought a 28-room mansion in Kenwood, two blocks from Nation of Islam leader, Elijah Muhammad.

During his early years on the South Side, Ali tried to blend in. He strolled alone underneath the "L" tracks, casually dressed in a button-down shirt and slacks. He hung out with friends at the automobile garage at 69th Street and Stony Island Boulevard. Often, he could be found at the Nation of Islam's bakery on 79th Street, flirting with the teenage waitress who would become his second wife.

"The most crucial time of his life was in Chicago," said Khalilah Camacho-Ali, a suburban Chicago native who married Ali in 1967. "These exile years were tough for him. He was growing and learning more about the religion. He was learning about life. All of this was during the struggle of the civil rights period, and he saw the rise of racism and the effect of racism on him."

It was in Chicago, according to those who knew him best, that the transformation from Cassius Clay to Muhammad Ali took shape. For nearly four years, he lived freely in Chicago while the appeal of his draft evasion conviction made its way to the U.S. Supreme Court. With a five-year jail sentence hanging over his head, he went toe to toe with adversity, turning down millions of dollars to stand up for what he believed was right.

On the South Side, people praised him for his courage. In many other places in the country, he was just another a draft dodger.

The 25-year-old Ali and his 17-year-old Muslim bride were married in a small ceremony at their home at 85th Street and South Jeffrey Boulevard in the South Shore neighborhood. The modest, two-bedroom brick bungalow, fully furnished and decorated in light blue, was a gift from the Nation of Islam.

Camacho-Ali said she and Ali, whom she divorced in 1977, lived as "regular people" in Chicago. But there were signs that this was no ordinary couple. Ali's heavyweight championship belt was displayed in a locked trophy case in the living room. Celebrities such as David Ruffin and other members of the Motown singing group the Temptations came by for dinner. And Ali drove around

Chicago in a red Cadillac convertible—a gift from his managers for winning a 1963 fight.

Ali's notoriety and conversion to Islam also brought unwelcome attention. The year before he married Camacho-Ali, the South Side apartment where he lived with his first wife was severely damaged in a suspicious fire. It occurred the same day that Ali's friend, Malcolm X, was shot to death in New York.

"Being a Muslim was a big controversy. In America, people objected to him belonging to a controversial group that was a nation within our own nation," said Camacho-Ali, who grew up in the Nation of Islam. "This stood against everything that his (Christian) mother and father believed in. These were young, tender times, and these were battlefields that he had to go through and learn from."

But for the most part, Ali could be himself on the South Side, she said.

"He was able to walk the streets of the South Side and be embraced. He felt support because the Muslims were watching his back 24/7. He felt comfortable where he was sitting. He felt comfortable in his life," his ex-wife said.

Initially, some within the nation questioned Ali's sincerity, said Salim Muwakkil, the former associate editor of the Nation of Islam's newspaper, *The Final Call.*

"Muhammad Ali was an aberration to a certain extent and it took a while for many of the more fervent members of the Nation of Islam to warm up to him," said Muwakkil, now a Chicago journalist and radio talk show host.

"They warmed up to him because Elijah Muhammad said he was good people. He was fully under the influence of the Nation of Islam. Still, he had to prove his passion for the Nation," said Muwakkil.

One way of showing his loyalty, according to Muwakkil, was to go on the speaking circuit. Ali traveled to college campuses from the University of Chicago to Howard University voicing his opposition to the war. He also became a minister in the Nation of Islam and spoke to massive crowds at the annual Savior's Day celebration in Chicago.

He was as vocal as Malcolm X when it came to the Nation of Islam, but people on the South Side were drawn to him for another reason.

"He was able to be both larger than life and completely down to earth simultaneously," said Chicago director Bill Siegel, whose 2014 documentary "The Trials of Muhammad Ali" documented Ali's four years out of the ring. "His ability to represent himself on an individual level and accept the role of being a symbol of defiance and courage is a huge part of his legacy."

While making the film, Siegel said he encountered many people who once had casual encounters with Ali in Chicago. One man remembered as a child sitting on Ali's lap at a Halloween party. A woman recalled the time she got a flat tire on the Dan Ryan Expressway and Ali pulled up in his Cadillac and fixed it for her, Siegel said.

Ali remained a pariah for much of official Illinois. Gov. Otto Kerner called Ali "unpatriotic." Mayor Richard J. Daley, though sympathetic to Elijah Muhammad and the thousands of potential voters he controlled, refused to call Ali by his Muslim name.

Except for winning the Golden Gloves title in Chicago in 1959, Ali never fought a bout in Chicago. By 1966, he had replaced his Louisville, Ky., management team with a Chicago-based group controlled by the Nation of Islam and headed by Elijah Muhammad's son, Herbert Muhammad. The anti-Muslim sentiment against him grew deeper.

That year, Ali was to defend his championship against Ernie Terrell in Chicago. But Daley, along with Kerner and other politicians, rescinded his Illinois boxing license so that the fight could not take place in Chicago and urged the Illinois Athletic Commission to cancel the bout altogether.

Ali was at a corner grocery store on 79th Street in 1971 when he heard that the Supreme Court had overturned his conviction. "I had just bought an orange when the owner came out and hugged me with tears in his eyes and told me I'd just been vindicated," Ali told reporters in a scene shown in the documentary.

After the ruling, the country's feelings toward Ali softened. Within a few years, Daley had made a complete turnaround. In 1974, after

Ali won the championship back from George Foreman, Daley held a reception for Ali at City Hall, where he praised him for "the things the champ stands for" and awarded him the city's Medal of Merit.

The proclamation read like a poem:

> "I Richard J. Daley, mayor of the city
> Do proclaim for this champion, clever and
> witty,
> For Muhammad Ali his own special day
> For receiving the honors he won the hard
> way."

Ali accepted gracefully. Nearly a decade after Daley refused him a boxing license, all was forgiven in his adopted hometown.

"I can't be angry with him," Ali told reporters. "Times have changed. I think Daley's changed."

~

"Muhammad Ali's exile years in Chicago: Learning about life," Dahleen Glanton, June 4, 2016. Licensed from the Chicago Tribune.

[NINE]

Ali vs. Marciano: The Fake Fight

By Ferdie Pacheco

Dr. Ferdie Pacheco was Ali's personal physician and cornerman from 1962 to 1977. In this excerpt, he describes Ali's fake fight against Rocky Marciano. The "fight" was created during Ali's exile years, after he was stripped of his boxing license. Pacheco refers to Chris and Angelo Dundee. Angelo was another of Ali's cornermen. His brother Chris Dundee ran Miami's famous Fifth Street Gym
—K.M.

Murray Woroner was a clever radio man who had a computerized script on the hour-by-hour birth of Christ. It played to a huge radio audience and won critical awards and financial rewards for him. Basking in the sunlight of critical acclaim, Murray looked for another project that would be suitable for turning into a computerized event.

It turned out that a spectacular possibility existed in

Fort Lauderdale, under his very nose. It was big. It was important. And it was, at that moment, financially feasible.

Rocky Marciano had retired undefeated and lived in Fort Lauderdale. Rocky was barely forty, and he was stewing in his juices to come back. The boxing commission said no, no, no. Stay undefeated, a hero to your people, with a place in boxing history. Rocky hated his manager, and that kept him from attempting a comeback. Still, Rocky wanted to fight.

Ali found himself in a hard place during his exile of 1967–70 when, because of his opposition to the Vietnam War, he became a conscientious objector. The main problem was that he was forbidden to fight—not even an exhibition in Miami or anywhere in the known world. As soon as the Black Muslims realized that Ali could no longer produce funds for them and then realized that Ali expected them to finance his retirement, they threw him out of the church, forbade him to ever use his Muslim name, and barred every mosque from permitting him to pray there. Muhammad Ali was shut out by his own people. It was disgraceful.

But Muhammad is a resilient man. He hears what he wants to hear. He kept on calling himself Muhammad Ali, and he went to any mosque he pleased: who would turn him away? He devised ways to make enough money to survive on his own, without the Muslims.

Probably none was more bizarre and creative than the suggestion that Murray Woroner came up with, which was the possibility of matching two undefeated champions to fight in a computer fight, which was fully legal. Wow! What a feature!

Chris and Angelo leapt at the chance. Marciano's people were tap dancing with joy. When he heard the story, Marciano began to diet and workout and ordered a new toupee.

The Muslims were furious, for they had cut themselves out of the loop. They were outside looking in, and their cash cow was ready to produce income for Murray Woroner but none for the Honorable Elijah Muhammad.

Murray was a genius in organizing the writing. He got himself a blue-ribbon panel of boxing experts, writers, fight people, and ex-boxers. They each submitted ideas on how a round would go, and Murray collated all the data through a master computer located in Birmingham, Alabama. This produced a shooting script, and they moved into a small movie studio for the filming. It would be a movie to be seen in theaters.

Angelo worked Ali's corner. Marciano had a friend, Mel Zeigler, help in his corner. He wanted no one known in boxing, at least, to carry his towel, spit bucket, and stool. But Marciano wouldn't need a known corner man. After all, it was a scripted film.

Rocky Marciano was a plain, wonderful, northern sort of Italian, with apparently hundreds of friends. He couldn't turn anyone down, except for money; Rocky was a cheapskate and hoarder of pennies. In fact, that was what caused his death. He was up north in Chicago. A friend called, asking Rocky to come to a relative's birthday party. He had a private plane and would pay $200 in cash. Rocky needed only to appear, shake a few hands, and catch a plane back to Florida, where his wife and child awaited. The plane crashed in a rainstorm in Newton, Iowa, and hit a tree; Rocky died. What a shame, for a measly $200.

Rocky had a love-hate thing going with Ali. He was convinced that in his prime, he would have beaten Ali. He just couldn't give Ali the credit the younger man deserved. He didn't think Ali was tough enough to stand up to the body blows of Marciano. Rocky had good reason for his high opinion of himself: he was undefeated at 49–0 (with 43 KO's). Even the great Joe Louis had caved in to his dreadful attack, and so had Archie Moore.

Rocky's main problem in boxing was not with opponents, it was his undying hatred of his manager, Al Weill. Weill was one of those detestable managers who thrived on denigrating his fighters by telling the press how dumb the boxer was, how he couldn't think for himself, and how he needed a keeper. Most of the time, he refused to call Rocky by name and used the old manager's moniker, "Fighter." And when referring to the fighter and the camp, it always came out "I." "I knocked out Archie Moore. I'm fighting Ezzard Charles." It was funny to the press. It wasn't funny to Marciano. Weill also cut in for a large percentage of the purse.

As Marciano grew into a top attraction and boxing men reluctantly conceded that Rocky Marciano was the greatest boxer in the world, Weill escalated his own fame and position.

The end came when Weill had the incredible chutzpah to actually slap Marciano in front of a full press conference. It was all Rocky could do not to knock Weill silly. Cooler heads prevailed, but Weill was out and Rocky, tied up by contracts while also hampered by a bad back, had no choice but to retire. His exit was applauded by his wife and daughter.

Many times during Sonny Liston's reign, Rocky, chafing at the bit and still a young man, wanted to come out of retirement, but the thought of making a dollar for Weill and his wife's insistence that he stay retired kept him at home.

While Rocky and the boxing world thought the huge, hard-punching Sonny Liston might be a stretch for the retired and flabby Marciano, no such caution was exhibited when Cassius Clay was mentioned. Men and boys. Then when Sonny was TKO'd by Muhammad Ali, Rocky saw red. He was sure that he could come out of retirement, train hard, and steamroll the kid. The thought of Weill benefiting kept Rocky at bay, though his restraint was killing him. He was sure that he could roll over Ali.

As far as Ali was concerned, he never studied opponents or fretted about who he was going to fight next. His philosophy, born of supreme self-confidence, was simply, "Bring 'em on. Whoever he is, I'll knock him out."

Ali never gave Rocky Marciano a thought as a possible opponent, because Marciano simply was not available. Why worry about an aging champion tied up in a bitter dispute with his manager and with a wife who wouldn't even consider a comeback? Rocky Marciano was simply not a consideration in his plans.

When he signed on for the computer fight, Ali was amused by the thought that people were around who still thought Rocky had a chance with him. "Even in his prime, Rocky had no chance with me. First thing, he is too little. Less than five foot ten to my six foot three inches. I'd overwhelm him, I'd lay on him in the clinches like a big old grizzly bear, and I'd smother his insides out. He was too small to reach me from outside. I'd jab him twenty to one. Rocky had a face that cut easily. Can you imagine what my stinging jab would do to those weak eyes? By round three, Rocky would look like he ran into a lawn mower. How could he beat me? No way, is how."

This was before three Frazier fights, three fights with Ken Norton, and the George Foreman fight proved Ali's hypothesis. Ali too big, Ali too fast, Ali too strong a puncher, Ali too fast a jab, and the bad news, Ali too tough, takes heavy punishment well. In the light of what we saw during his long career, I'm afraid Ali was right. Marciano, while a formidable opponent, wouldn't have lasted long.

Oh, I know. Every time I speak at the Sons of Italy banquets, I get hooted down.

"Look what Rocky done to Ali in that fight they had! He beat Ali," they would yell in my face.

"Well, yes and no. In your city, Rocky won. In Ali's city, Chicago, Louisville, et cetera, Ali won. In some it was a draw. In some Rocky lost on a cut, et cetera.

"Fellers, it was a filmed fight, a fake. They wrote it. It was a scripted fight. They needed fifteen rounds. They wrote fifteen rounds."

I'm amazed by the public perception of that fight. I watched it in the Miami Beach Auditorium along with Chris and Angelo. People rushed to me after the fight. The press put microphones in my face:

"How bad was the cut?"

"How many stitches did it take to stop it?"

"When can he fight again?"

"Did the cut retire Rocky again?"

"Fellers, it was a fake fight," I had to say. "It was a scripted fight filmed in a studio with no audience. The cut was fake with fake blood, do you understand? Like actors in a movie."

No one listened. Boy, what a job we did with that fight.

But they wouldn't listen. That's what they saw with their own eyes, and their thinking went like this: "I don't care what anyone says, Rocky got cut real bad. And the only reason he lost was the cut."

Even today, people persist in feeling that the fight was real. While writing this book, I spoke to several expert sportswriters who argued violently that Marciano had beaten Ali in a fifteen-round decision. They refused to believe that Ali won in Ali-land.

"Yeah, in Miami, you're right. In Chicago it was Ali. In most of Europe, except of course Italy, it was Ali."

They seemed mortified that they were cheated, flimflammed. "Fix," they wanted to scream. "But it's a movie," we would answer. Years later, the Black Muslims decided they needed a biography about Ali. They sent Ali with Richard Durham (who, in Ali's camp, was known as "Hemingway") to interview Murray Woroner. Woroner refused to see him, for not only had he spent his profits trying to get the then-banned Ali a title fight, but also he was getting flogged in the black press by favoring Marciano. They saw it as a racist trick.

Ali asked me to arrange an interview at Murray's house. I assured Murray that it would be fine; they were just writing the story of the computerized fight with Marciano. Murray's wife, who had responded badly to the racist slurs they were receiving, had to be cooled off.

As we approached the pool, Ali whispered to me, "Stay out of this, Doc, we don't want your name in this." Uh-oh. I could see that Durham had come loaded for bear. He whipped out a tape recorder and had twenty racist questions for the amazed Woroner, such as this:

"Where was the computer used to write the script?"

"Birmingham."

"That's in Alabama?" Durham narrowed his eyes and looked conspiratorially at Ali. "In the South. How many white guys on the board of experts?" Durham asked.

"About fifty-fifty. We had big names like Sugar Ray Robinson, Joe Louis, and those guys." Murray started getting the drift that they were there to sandbag him.

This was the height of chutzpah. Murray Woroner was a very liberal man who had supported black causes during the days of segregation.

Although he forbade his children to use the "n— word" in his house, here were Ali and Durham screaming it at every turn. It was downright embarrassing to be there. Soon Murray finished the interview in which he had been reviled and accused of blatant racism. His wife was livid. I had my head down.

Nonplussed, Ali put his arm around Murray as we walked to the car.

"Say, bossman," said Ali, turning Uncle Tom before our disbelieving eyes, "you think you can advance me two hundred dollars out of your advances?"

"I don't carry that kind of money in my bathing suit," said Murray through clenched teeth.

"Ask your wife," said Ali innocently.

"I don't think so," I said, taking him by the arm and putting him in my car.

"This is the kind of stuff we need," said Durham happily.

The injustice of that horrible afternoon was that Ali had benefited the most from the computer fight. It kept his name alive. It showed him boxing again. It made him a nice sum of money right at the time that he was down with nobody showing up to lend him a helping hand. It brought Ali to the front again as an employable name. Campus dates and speaking dates followed. Murray Woroner's wonderful idea had legitimized Ali as a commodity once again and saved his financial life. It was a huge plus!

Murray Woroner took the interview very hard, for he, like all who came under Ali's spell, had come to believe that he was somehow part of Ali's inside family. He wasn't, he couldn't be, for he was white.

Not long after, Murray Woroner had his last heart attack and died. Soon after, so did his wife.

What had started out as a joyful, fun-filled event to help out Ali turned into a sad major tragedy.

What a shame.

As to the filming of the fight, it was enjoyable and basically uneventful. Three 8-hour days, in and out; it was easy.

Regardless of the script, Rocky seemed unable to pull his punches, whereas Ali could come within a fraction of an inch to making it look extremely real. Our problem was that Ali was getting madder and madder as Rocky thumped one hard shot after another off his ribs.

By the end of the second day, Ali stopped the filming to have a word with Rocky.

"Rocky, you're supposed to be pulling those body shots. You aren't, and they're hurting my ribs. Now, if we're going to have a real fight, then you will not be able to land those shots without me peppering your face with hard left jabs and right hooks, and if you do by chance land a body shot, you're going to take back a stinging right hand to the nose to break it again. Now, do we play movie or do we play boxing?"

By the last three rounds, they quit trying to pull their punches and let fly. Watch those rounds closely. That's more like it would have been. That alone was worth money.

Marciano knew he was wrong. Secretly, he wanted to find out if Ali could take his best body shots. To his surprise, he found that Ali could. End of the problem.

I had a lot of fun showing a round or two when I went on a speaking tour. A curious thing happened. I would show a couple of rounds of the first or second Ali-Liston fight and then the filmed fight. Without exception, the audience always got excited about the fake fight and wanted to see more. The real fight wasn't as exciting.

I found that a nice justification for the job Murray Woroner did in writing, staging, and shooting the two undefeated champions in a steamy little studio in South Miami.

Too bad Murray did not get the credit due to him or the money he should have made with proper distribution.

If you don't take away anything else from this chapter, let me reiterate. Commit this to memory.

1. It was a movie that followed a script.
2. There were thirteen endings, depending on where it was shown.
3. The cut was bogus.

4.Ali would have beaten Marciano if they had ever really fought.

"When Ali took on Marciano," in Tales from the 5th Street Gym: Ali the Dundees and Miami's Golden Age of Boxing, by Ferdie Pacheco. Gainesville: University Press of Florida, 2010, pp. 108–116. Reprinted with permission from the University Press of Florida.

[TEN]

Ali and the Supreme Court

By The Washington Times Staff

More than three decades after the Supreme Court cleared Ali, The Washington Post looked back at the event. (The story contains a minor error. Ali's fight against Jerry Quarry was held in Atlanta, not New York.) —K.M.

~

The former heavyweight champion of the world heard the news as he was leaving a store on Chicago's South Side after buying an orange.

"The fellow who owns the store ran out of the store and grabbed me while I was getting into my car," the boxer told newsmen later in the day. "He hugged me and said, 'I just heard the news on the radio—you're free! You're free!'"

Thirty-four years ago tomorrow, Muhammad Ali indeed was free—and for good. Saying his "beliefs are founded on tenets of the Muslim religion as he understands them," the court had overturned the government's 1967 conviction of Ali, who had been sentenced to five years in prison for refusing induction into the Army as a conscientious objector. The court's ruling was by unanimous decision, words familiar to boxing fans, with Justice Thurgood Marshall abstaining because he had been solicitor general for the Justice Department while it was prosecuting Ali.

In its ruling, the Court held that a conscientious objector must be against war in any form, must show his objection is based on religious training and must show it is sincere. It said the Justice Department "was simply wrong as a matter of law in advising that the petitioner's beliefs were not religiously based and were not sincerely held."

Asked how he would celebrate his legal victory, Ali replied, "I've done my celebrating already. I said a prayer to Allah." Then he left to resume training for a fight with Jimmy Ellis, a former sparring partner, the following month in Houston.

As soon as the news reached the public, Ali was cheered or cussed anew throughout the nation as a hero or traitor, according to each person's lights.

Around the world, however, untold thousands celebrated. Many were black, but race was unimportant here. Rejoicing just as heartily were others who believed the United States' involvement in the constantly escalating war in Vietnam was unwise and unjust.

Love him or hate him—and almost nobody was neutral—Ali had stood up for what he believed regardless of personal cost. The battle, his toughest ever, had started more than four years earlier when his number came up at Selective Service.

In the tense mid-1960s, Cassius Clay/Muhammad Ali was a controversial figure. Childish poetry and braggadocio had marked his ascent to the heavyweight title, won in February 1964 when the supposedly invincible Sonny Liston refused to come out for the seventh round of their bout in Miami Beach. The following day, "Clay" announced he was changing his name and converting to the Nation of Islam.

Fifteen months later, he knocked out Liston in the first round at

Lewiston, Maine, with a "phantom punch" that looked more like a slap, and cries of "fix" rent the air. Later when Ali showed unusual cruelty while beating up clean-cut former champion Floyd Patterson, whom he deemed an "Uncle Tom," many fans turned away.

Drafted for the Army in 1967, Ali went into a figurative rope-and-dope. "I ain't got no quarrel with them Viet Cong," he said famously if ungrammatically. "No Viet Cong ever called me [the 'n' word]."

On April 28, protesters repeatedly shouted, "Draft beer, not Ali," as they gathered outside the U.S. Veterans Administrative Office in Houston, where the boxer was scheduled to report for induction.

Inside the building, a lieutenant ordered the most famous of 46 draftees to step forward, barking, "Cassius Clay—Army!"

Ali didn't move.

"Clay—Army!" the officer said again.

Ali stood still.

Another officer faced Ali and explained the penalty for refusing induction: five years' imprisonment and a $10,000 fine. Told he would have to state his objection in writing, Ali quickly scribbled, "I refuse to be inducted . . . because I claim to be exempt as a minister of the religion of Islam."

Soon after, Ali was stripped of his title, sentenced to prison and fined. Appeals by his attorneys kept him out of a cell, but he remained idle in the ring for what would have been 3 prime years of his career—ages 25 to 28. Finally, New York State granted him a license to fight, and he knocked out veteran trial horse Jerry Quarry on Oct.26, 1970.

Then came the first of three epic fights against champion Joe Frazier, which Ali lost by decision on March8, 1971—his first defeat in 32 bouts. He fought on for another 10 years—most notably against Frazier, George Foreman and Ken Norton—trying to make up for lost time and taking countless punches to the head that eventually left him with Parkinson's syndrome. After losses to Leon Spinks, Larry Holmes and Trevor Berbick, Ali retired in December 1981 at age 39.

As his fighting skills declined, Ali remained a hero to millions because of the same courage he had shown that day long ago in

Houston. After his retirement, he continued to be venerated as the Parkinson's slowed his speech and movements. Wherever he went, he was hailed as "Champ" or simply "Ali." Today he arguably remains the world's most recognizable figure inside or outside of sports.

In 1996, he appeared seemingly out of nowhere as the unannounced torch bearer who ignited the Olympic cauldron to begin the Atlanta Games—and his slow progress made millions weep.

Bryant Gumbel described the occasion perfectly in ESPN Classic's "Sports Century" series: "If you had told somebody in 1968 that Muhammad Ali [today] would be the most beloved individual on Earth and the mere sight of him holding an Olympic torch would bring people to tears, you'd have won a lot of bets."

~

"Ali had Supreme Court in his corner in 1971," June 27, 2005. Licensed from The Washington Times.

[ELEVEN]

Ali vs. Frazier I: "The Fight of the Century"

By Muhammad Ali with Richard Durham

In this excerpt from Muhammad Ali's 1975 biography, he remembers his first fight against Joe Frazier. It is 1971 and this this is Ali's third fight after returning from "exile." He is still undefeated as a professional boxer. In the excerpt, Ali goes back and forth between his pre-match bravado and the realities of the fight. It begins minutes before the fight and then picks up in the sixth round when Joe Frazier comes out fast, direct and hard.

—K.M.

~

I put my prediction on TV: the cameras were shooting me for the closed-circuit audience. I gave them a special message: my predictions of how the fight would end. I predicted the sixth round, gave it to them in a sealed envelope which they were to open only five minutes before the fight. I wanted it that way so there'd be no late betting on it. "Here I am, five minutes before the fight and predictin'. If I were a Patterson or Terrell or Chuvalo or any other fighter, I would be praying or shadowboxing at this time, but I'm putting it down on paper. I'm putting it on record for all to see." In the envelope were my words:

It won't even be close!
Joe will look like an amateur!
And I will be the pro!
I'm going to shuffle and jab and clinch and holler,
And I'll have a good time for four or five rounds
Before I really get serious.
I predict Frazier will fall in Round Six!

Joe knows what I predicted and he comes out fast, direct, hard. His head bobbing and weaving, his neck on a swivel. I jab and shoot straight rights at him. I hook him and he pushes me toward the corner. I lay back on the ropes again, and his left explodes against my hips, my ribs. Then he brings it up to my head and I seem paralyzed. I don't hit back. I lay on the ropes, and the crowd is booing . . . . Joe has opened the round with a hook to my jaw that stuns me. Now he tries to move in for an uppercut. I shoot sharp jabs to his head and try to move him back, but he's pushing, driving like he's a tank. He's smashing at me on the ropes. His arms are short, stubby, and he can hit at close range with awful power. I try to move back, but he pins me against the ropes and he's throwing bombs. The crowd is up and screaming, "Joe! Joe! Come on, Joe!" They think he's close to a victory, and they've never seen me this way before. They're yelling, "Joe! Joe! Joe! Joe!" He's throwing punches and they're landing. Something has gone out of me; I feel tired and the fight is not half over. I know from experience that if I hold on, I will grow stronger. But the air in my lungs is hot, my arms are heavy. I look out at the crowd. I think how the world is watching. I've got to do what I said I would do.

I had forecast: I'm gonna say to Smokin' Joe, "Come on, Joe. Let's smoke!" I'm gonna reach him because my arms are longer. I'm faster and when I hit, it's gonna be devastating. It's gonna be sharp. His body punches ain't that bad. Body punches never really could kill anybody. I'm gonna say, "Come on, Joe. You can do better. Joe, you ain't smokin' at all."

But he is smokin'. I think I take the seventh, but in the eighth, Joe drives on, moves on, pushes on, falls on, but keeps coming on. I jab him, straight sharp jabs. He moves me against the ropes. I give him light, sharp jabs. My weariness is greater now. I wonder if Joe Louis is right about those three and a half years. When I lay on the ropes, the crowd boos, and yells for Joe to take me out.

The bell rings. I go back to my corner. I've got to turn the fight around.

The ninth comes, and I feel my strength returning. When Joe comes in, I catch him with a sharp right. He staggers me with a hook, but I'm shooting straight rights to his head, and they're beginning to connect. All of a sudden, everything comes into focus. I'm not missing any more. He's bleeding from the left nostril. He staggers. I'm putting it together again! He's backing up! I land six, seven, eight straight solid rights to his head. There's a lump over his eye the size of a coffee cup, getting bigger and bigger with each blow I land. But he keeps coming in, keeps coming in, but now I'm ready for him. Everything I throw hits! When the round ends, he's bleeding above the eye, from his nose and mouth. But he won't go down. Now I know he'll die before he quits.

I told the fans, the crowd that came around the gym each day: "I'll come out and touch his nose with my fist." I stand up in the ring and demonstrate how I'll hold his head at a distance. I'll talk to him: "Let's get it on, Joe! I'm gonna whip you and all those white folks who are backing you. Boy, you in trouble tonight! Joe, you won't land a blow. So you set up a victory party? Duke Ellington's gonna play at your party, you say? NO! No! No! Not tonight, Joe! You won't have no victory party tonight. You'll be coming to my victory party. I'm gonna have a party for you when this is all over, Joe. In round ten, if you still in the ring, I'm gonna tag you and tame you like you was a pussy cat. You ain't the monster the press make you out to be. You'll see by round ten."

Joe is on top of me and I feel his left hook against my jaw. I'm holding my hands up high, but he gets through. I shoot lefts and rights to his head, but he digs his fist into my ribs. His chin is on my chest. I know why he's moving with such force, why he's so fierce in this round. Yank Durham predicted that I would go in the tenth round. My back is against the ropes and he's pressing hard. The same exhaustion I felt earlier comes down on me. I'm missing again. The tight focus I had in the last round is gone. Still I catch him coming in with a straight left. I hook and throw a right, and it blunts him. And in the clinch for the first time, I feel his heavy breathing. The pace is killing me, but it's killing him, too.

The bell. The round is over, both of our predictions failed. I just manage a slight edge. But I've got five rounds to recover. I've done it before, I can do it now.

When he throws a punch at me, I'm gonna shake my head and say, "Man, you ain't landing a blow!" Then I'm gonna do a little shuffle and I'm gonna hit him—BAM! and say, "You know you don't stand a chance, sucker." I'm gonna clinch with him. I'm gonna have a ball. If the sucker's still crazy, I got a new punch, the Ali Ghetto Ripper. I'm gonna lay it on him in the eleventh. If it goes that far.

I come out determined to win the eleventh, twelfth, thirteenth. And I want the remaining ones. Frazier is bobbing, weaving, more confident than ever. Suddenly he dips under my right and comes up with the hardest hook I've ever taken in my life. It flung me back across the ring. I'm almost out on my feet. My head is numb and I see him coming, but I jab and back off. There's water on the floor and I slip, but there's no count. I get back up, but in the next round he comes out again, throwing himself recklessly, taking blows that bounce off his head, off his chin, off his face. His mouth is bleeding. In the twelfth and thirteenth, I stay away and throw punches, long-range. They cut into his head, but he presses on, crowding me. He'll take three, four, five, six punches to get a solid shot at my body, at the hips, at the head. There's something about the way he comes in, bobbing, weaving, that throws me off. He's easy to hit; then he's not easy to hit. I've never fought anyone with a will so strong. He's human, I think, so it's got to be hurting him. His left eye is swollen. His right eye is cut. His lips are torn as though they are going to drop off. I'm throwing jabs and scoring, but he's still moving in. I get by the fourteenth. Just one more to go.

I walk down 146th and Broadway. Pedestrians forget where they are going and follow me. Traffic is blocked. People pour out into the streets, and I cry out, "Where's Joe Frazier! Where's the White Folks' Champion! When I git him in the ring, you'll see. There'll be no contest."

I've been building up this fight since I was in exile. It'll be the biggest fight in history. Greater than when David fought Goliath, greater than when Grant took Richmond, greater than when any two men ever fought each other on the planet Earth. I'll be whipping the people that took my title and gave it to him.

Red Smith says the build-up started long ago: "It goes back to the days when Clay's posturing and preening and rancid verse and self-praise began to make total strangers yearn to see him stopped with a fistful of knuckles. Frazier is the first candidate conceded a chance to accomplish this."

But Red is wrong if he thinks Frazier will be the victor. I'll close the book on all the fighters. If Joe Frazier whips me, I'm gonna crawl across the ring, and say, "Joe, if you whip me, you the real Champion of the World. I'm gonna crawl across the ring and look up at you and say, 'You the real Champ of the World.'"

The Garden is on its feet. Only a few shout, "Ali! Ali! Ali! Ali!" But Frazier's supporters are confident and loud: "Joe! Come on, Joe! Knock him out, Joe! Knock him out, Joe!"

He's moving into range. I want to circle, jab and come through with a straight right. I see an opening. I move toward it, then I see him dip. He dips and leaps up with his left, almost from the floor. I see it coming. I think I can ride it back. But he has it timed to perfection. It explodes against my head and I don't remember going down. Only being down. Looking up and hearing the count, and knowing I had no business being down. I get up and take the count. The roars from the crowd are in my ear. "Joe! Joe! Joe! Joe! Joe Frazier!"

"That's the blow that did it, that blew out the candles," Bundini will tell me later.

I jab and tie him up, hold him off, keep him from following up. When the bell rings and before I go back to my corner, I see his face is a mass of blood and lumps, swollen, but so is mine. My jaw is swollen to the size of a melon. Halfway through the fight, Angelo thought it was broken. As I stand back in my corner and wait for the verdict, all my bones ache. My hips feel like they've been beaten by baseball bats.

"The winner by unanimous decision, undisputed World Heavyweight Champion, Joe Frazier!"

People are pouring into the ring past the police. I move behind Bundini and Angelo to the steps until I feel somebody pulling my arm, making me turn around. Joe has come over to my corner. "You put up a great fight," he says. His face is so swollen I can hardly see his eyes, but I know he's looking at me.

"You The Champ," I say.

He seems to like that. It's the first time as a pro that I have to acknowledge another man over me. I had promised to crawl across the ring and say, "You a bad nigger."

Joe seems to read my mind. Blood is seeping from the cuts in his lips. "We don't do no crawling," he says. "You fought one helluva fight. You one bad nigger. We both bad niggers. We don't do no crawling."

People are pushing past me to get to shake hands with The Champion.

"How do you feel?" An announcer is pushing a microphone up to me, but I move past him. I don't tell him that my first feeling is relief. I'm glad it's over.

~

[TWELVE]

Ali's Greatest Rival

By Thom Loverro

Thom Loverro is a sports columnist for the Washington Times.

The magnitude of Muhammad Ali, the social change warrior, is so great that in his passing, it has overshadowed the greatness of Muhammad Ali, the heavyweight champion.

There have been plenty of video clips of his fights shown on various networks this week, but they seem to serve as the platform to talk about how Ali touched so many people.

It says something about your place in history when you are the greatest heavyweight champion in the history of boxing and that is not the greatest impact you had on the world during your time on Earth.

He was the greatest heavyweight champion. It is often a two-fighter debate, between Ali and Joe Louis, who held the title from 1937 to 1949 and, like Ali when he fought Joe Frazier the first time, fought in a "Fight of the Century" that had far-reaching implications beyond the ring when he knocked out German heavyweight Max Schmeling in 1938 as the world was about to go to war.

Louis successfully defended his heavyweight title 26 times. He was ranked the best heavyweight of all time by the International Boxing Research Organization in 2005. But, Ali fought during the golden age of heavyweights—the 1960s and 1970s—and the quality of opponents he faced, from Frazier to George Foreman to Ken Norton in seven of his 61 fights, was greater than the opponents that Louis faced.

There was one guy, though, that may have been greater than Ali—or, at the very least, was Ali's greatest rival in the ring. No, it wasn't Frazier, Foreman or Norton.

It was the diminutive, quiet man who stood in the corner and faced Ali seven times during the champion's career, and trained both of the fighters who gave Ali the most trouble—the legendary trainer Eddie Futch, who once sparred with Joe Louis in Detroit in the early 1930s.

Futch had Ali's number, and Ali knew it. At a ceremony at City Hall in New York nearly 30 years ago that included Ali, Foreman, Frazier and Larry Holmes, Ali said to Futch, "You always gave me trouble."

Yes, he did.

It was Futch who developed the strategy for Frazier to defeat Ali in their historic 1971 meeting.

"Ali was a great fighter, and he was in my mind even greater than what most people thought he was, because he had limited ability and he made that work," Futch, who passed away in 2001 at the age of 90, once told me. "Ali hardly ever threw a body punch. He never ducked a punch. He always pulled back or away from a punch, blocked it or slipped it.

"I charted Ali's strengths—the things he was a master at—and I also charted the things that he couldn't do. So, I set up our strategy to avoid his strengths as much as we possibly could and to exploit his weaknesses as much as we possibly could.

"One of them was that he could not throw the right-hand upper cut properly, so we had Joe bob and weave in a more exaggerated way, just a little lower than he normally did, and stayed close so he could work the body and to watch for Ali's right hand to drop to throw the uppercut.

"Ali is going to have to dig him out of that low stance with punches coming up. He would try to dig Joe out of that stance, and he would have to do it with the uppercut. He would stand up straight and didn't bend his knees, didn't bend his body to throw the uppercut.

"So, I told Joe, 'The minute you see his right hand come down, you throw the left. He's got nothing up there. You can catch them with the left.' The only time that you hit Ali was when he is punching. When he throws the uppercut, you throw the hook. That's the punch that hurt [Ali] so badly in the 11th round and that's the punch that knocked him down in the 15th round.

"Ali was throwing the uppercut and Joe threw the hook. I had worked on that round after round after round, telling Joe to step in and throw that hook when he saw the right hand come down. The battle plan was carried out, to bob and weave and stay low and stay in close, stay tight and to work the body and make him bring his hands down. And then [Frazier] shifted to the head when [Ali] brought them down."

Futch was in the corner for the three Ali/Frazier fights—he was the man who refused to let Frazier, nearly blinded, come out for the 15th and final round in their 1975 "Thrilla in Manila" bout. Futch told me that the betrayal Frazier, who helped Ali while he was banned from boxing from 1967 to 1970 for his refusal to enter the Army after being drafted during the Vietnam War, felt at the hands of Ali, who publicly ridiculed Frazier, was real and deep.

"Joe resented it when Ali started making all those personal attacks on him to hype the gate at the fights," Futch said. "He didn't think that was necessary. He felt betrayed because he had helped Ali. There were occasions when Ali would call and ask if he should come to one of Joe's fights, or would it be better for him to stay away, things like that. They were working together to get Ali reinstated."

During that time, Futch was also working with an unknown heavyweight in California—an ex-Marine named Norton.

While Ali was exiled from boxing, he would travel around to boxing gyms around the country and find heavyweights to spar with him. One day, he entered the Hoover Street Gym in Los Angeles, where Futch was training Norton. After sparring with three heavyweights, Ali asked if anyone else was up for a sparring session. Someone told him Futch had a heavyweight that might be worthy of sparring with the deposed champion.

Ali asked Futch if his man was up for it, and Futch said yes. "I had been waiting for him to make the suggestion," he said.

The gym had already filled up when word spread of Ali's appearance. Futch pulled Norton aside before he got in the ring and told him, "Don't be a smart guy. Go in there and try to learn something. Just go along and work with him, don't try anything cute. But if he tries to take advantage of you, take care of yourself."

Norton did just that when he first began sparring with Ali, but with the gym filling up, Ali wanted to put on a show. So, before the second round started, Ali declared loudly, "OK, boy, I'm through playing with you. I'm going to put something on you now."

Futch told Norton, "OK, now take care of yourself."

Ali didn't realize that Norton was stronger than perhaps any fighter he had ever faced. Ali tried to back Norton into a corner, and Norton picked him up and threw him into the corner. The crowd laughed, and Ali was embarrassed, Futch said. Ali thought he had simply lost his balance, so he tried to back Norton into a corner again, and again Norton manhandled him. The crowd went crazy.

"Now it developed into a war," Futch said.

They started throwing hard right hands at each other. Ali threw a right hand a little too long, and Norton pulled away and nailed Ali with a hard right counterpunch. "Now the crowd is really into, yelling and screaming," Futch said. "The place was wild."

They went at each other for another minute, and the bell sounded to end the round. Ali left the gym, but returned the next day, screaming, "I want that Norton! I want that Norton!"

Futch told Norton, "Don't put your stuff on." Ali kept yelling, and asked Futch, "What's the matter, isn't he fighting today?"

Futch said he told Ali, "Yesterday, you came in looking for a workout. Today, you came in looking for a fight. When this kid fights you, he's going to get paid for it."

Norton did, several years later, and, while Ali officially won two of their three bouts, most observers believe Norton won the third and final fight at Yankee Stadium in 1976.

Boxing greatest is measured by the tests that you face from opponents in the ring. If Ali was truly "The Greatest," Futch helped make him great.

~

"Of all of Muhammad Ali's rivals, perhaps his greatest was Eddie Futch," Thom Loverro, June 7, 2016. Licensed from The Washington Times.

[THIRTEEN]

The Poetry of Muhammad Ali

By Victor Bockris

Victor Bockris spent time with Muhammad Ali in 1973 and 1974 at "In Fighter's Heaven," Ali's private training camp. At the time, Ali was training for the "Rumble in the Jungle" fight against George Foreman. In this excerpt, Ali shares his poetry with the writer.
—K.M.

~

One spring morning at eleven o'clock, I was standing in front of the kitchen, waiting for Ali to appear from the gym where he was taking a shower after his five-mile morning run. Suddenly the screen door to the gym swung open with a creak, we turned and: 'Over here fella!' Ali called out and ducked back inside the cabin, leaving the door ajar. I ran across the courtyard and stepped through the door.

Ali was standing naked in the entrance to the shower, drying himself off with a small bath towel. He wasn't as tall as I had expected, but the nakedness was startling, and after saying hello and shaking hands, I sat down on the rumpled day-bed and waited for him to get dressed.

Continuing to dry himself, Ali asked me what I wanted to talk about. I reminded him that I had called to talk about his poetry, and Ali seemed pleased by the idea. 'All these people who come to see me,' he was saying, 'they just want to hear more of the same old stuff—I'm the greatest! I'm the prettiest fighter!' He raised his arms and stood naked in the doorway with a defiant look on his face. But I don't want to do that anymore, he continued, rubbing his arms slowly. 'They wanted me to be professor of poetry at Oxford. Some people don't understand it, but . . .' and his words trailed off as he looked away.

Slowly, deliberately, he began to get dressed, pulling on a pair of brown trousers, a blue velours top, and the heavy hiking boots he wears at all times while training. There was another long silence, and then the telephone rang. Ali leaned across the bed and pulled the phone off the hook.

'Yeah?' he said in a low, soft voice. 'Yeah, okay. Well yeah. You do that. Okay. We'll see you. Goodbye.' This was the first of many phonecalls he was to answer personally, both when I called and when I was with him at the camp. At other times, for no apparent reason, he would refuse to come to the phone. This, coupled with the fact that there were never any bodyguards evident at the camp, surprised me. Ali has known some people, ranging from Malcolm X to Major Coxson of the Philadelphia 'Black Mafia,' who have been assassinated. Many people dislike him, others hate him, and even more are eager to use him. He receives a constant stream of requests for interviews and endorsements of every kind. Still, he often answers his own telephone and always leaves his doors unlocked.

Ali swung his legs back over the day-bed and stood up. 'Let me put this thing away,' he said, pointing down toward the bed. I got up and watched him fold the brown army blanket carefully before placing the bed against the wall. Then he sat in a straight-backed chair beside the door leading out to the gym.

For a full minute I waited for him to speak, watching him, but he was staring at the floor, distracted, as if I wasn't even in his room. Finally he slid his right hand up under his shirt, pulling the shirt up and revealing a layer of fat around his waist. He looked up and caught me staring at him. 'Gotta lose this,' he said, rubbing his stomach in a circular motion, staring back at the floor. 'No drinking, no women, I got fresh air up here, fresh air up here, fresh water, vegetables, you can breathe . . .

'Gotta lose this,' he said again, standing up and walking toward the door. 'Come on, we'll go over to the kitchen.' I followed him into the courtyard. As he strode ahead, he suddenly stopped, his fists at waist level, danced three steps, threw a quick punch into the air, and settled back into a walk again. I followed him into the kitchen.

'See that sign?' he asked, stopping in the center of the cafeteria and pointing to the far wall. 'My father painted it. He's painted all the signs up here.' He crossed to the coffee machines: 'Help yourself,' he said, without turning around.

I took a seat at one of the long tables, and Ali began talking about the origins of his poetry.

'It was '62, when I fought Archie Moore. Moore rhymed with four, so the publicity for that fight was:

> Moore will
> hit the floor
> in round four

Then I fought Henry Cooper, I said:

> This is no jive
> Cooper will
> leave in five

One thing led to another.' As the conversation progressed, Ali became increasingly absorbed, rocking back and forth in his metal chair, bringing his fist down on the table to establish a point, laughing, smiling, frowning in mock ferocity as he read his fight poems. Then suddenly he switched off, slowed down and, gazing past me, explained: 'But I don't write these boxing poems much anymore. Sometimes I write poems now, but they're different. I just wrote a freedom poem, goes like this:

Freedom

Better far, from all I see,
To die fighting to be free.
What more fitting end could be?

Better surely than in some bed,
Where in broken health I'm led,
Lingering until I'm dead.

Better than with cries and pleas
Or in the clutch of some disease,
Wastin' slowly by degrees.
Better than of heart attack
Or some dose of drug I lack,
Let me die by being black.

Better far that I should go
Standing here against the foe.
Is there sweeter death to know?
Better than the bloody stain
On some highway where I'm lain,
Torn by flyin' glass and pain.

Better call on death to come
Than to die another dumb
Looted victim in the slum.

Better than of prison rot,
If there's any choice I've got,
Rather perish on the spot.

Better now my fight to wage,
Now while my blood boils with rage,
Less it cool with ancient age.

Better valid for me to die
Than to Uncle Tom and try
Making peace just to live a lie.

Better if I say my sooth,
I'm gonna die demandin' truth
While I'm still akin to youth.

Better now than later on,
Now that the fear of death is gone,
Never mind another dawn.

'Bad!' he swore softly, looking across at me. He had been reciting from memory. 'These are some of the things I don't reveal to the public too much. Here's another. This poem is entitled "Truth":

Truth

The face of truth is open
The eyes of truth are bright
The lips of truth are never closed
The head of truth is upright.

The breath of truth stands forward
The gaze of truth is straight
Truth has neither fear nor doubt
Truth has patience to wait.

The words of truth are touching
The voice of truth is deep
The law of truth is simple
All that you sew *(sic)* you reap.

The soul of truth is flaming
The heart of truth is warring
The mind of truth is clear
And firm through rain and storm.

Facts are but its shadow
Truth stands above all sin
Great be the battle of life
Truth in the end shall win.

The image of truth is Elijah Muhammad
Wisdom's message his rod
The sign of truth is the crescent
The soul of truth is God.

The life of truth is eternal
Immortal is its past
Truth has the power to endure
Truth shall always last.

'That's my masterpiece,' he said, and slumped back in his chair.

After a couple of minutes—during which Ali rubbed his stomach and looked out of the window—I asked him how he found the time to write. 'During the night sometimes,' he said.

~

[FOURTEEN]

Ali vs. Foreman: "The Rumble in the Jungle"

By George Foreman

After losing his first match versus Joe Frazier in 1971, Ali was able to extract revenge with a win in 1974. But by then, Frazier was no longer world champion. He'd lost the title to George Foreman in 1973. A match against Foreman would give Ali another chance to regain what was stripped of him during the exile years. But it wouldn't be easy. Foreman had never been defeated in his professional career. In the following excerpt, Foreman describes the famous Rumble in the Jungle title fight in Kinshasa, Zaire.
—K.M.

Don King had come to me before the Norton fight. "I can put you together with Muhammad Ali," he said.

"Are you sure?"

He said yes.

I called Ali myself to check. "Do you want to fight me?" I asked.

"Yep."

"You're sure?"

"Yep."

Though he said yes, I thought I perceived some hesitation in his voice.

The next time I talked to Don King he claimed he could get me five million dollars for the fight. That was an extraordinary amount of money, beyond anything I could have imagined. The previous highest purse had been the five million split evenly between Ali and Joe Frazier for their second fight, held in January 1974. "Will you do it?" he asked.

"You sign this piece of paper right here," I said. " 'Five million dollars for George Foreman.' Then you've got me."

He came back in a few days. "Muhammad wants five million also," he said.

"Go ahead, give it to him," I said. "I don't care what he gets, so long as I get my five."

I had a feeling Ali wouldn't have fought for less—not as a matter of honor, but because he was afraid of me. He got more afraid, I'm sure, after the Norton fight. Word later came through Don King that the Muslims, on behalf of Ali, were upset. They requested that I stop saying I would kill him. Everyone could see that I meant what I was saying, and that upset them. They asked me respectfully to cool it, because, "you know, Ali's kind of old for boxing. Please."

"Well," I said, "since it's a religious request, I won't say that I'm going to kill him. I'll just say that I'm going to knock him out—in a hurry."

The next time I saw Ali was at the boxing writers' annual banquet, where I was to receive the "Fighter of the Year" award and my W.B.A. championship belt. They'd invited him to be guest speaker. Before we arrived, I told Mr. Moore that I planned to get on Muhammad somehow the same way he always seemed to be pulling stupid practical jokes on others. "I'm gonna tear his coat off."

I'd once run into Ernie Terrell, the boxer who was most famous for refusing to accept Cassius Clay's name as Muhammad Ali. "You can whip that guy, but you've got to watch out for the Muslims," he'd said, claiming that a few days before their fight, he answered his hotel door. A group of men in bow ties ran in, picked up every item that wasn't nailed down, put everything down again, and ran out. "Those are the games they play. They do strange things."

I sat back on the dais, watching Muhammad clowning around behind the podium, snug and smug in his element. These reporters were his prime audience. They loved and appreciated him. His quickness with words made their jobs easier. Me, I grunted and growled. You could have put all my quotable quotes on the head of a pin and still had room left for my sense of humor.

"And now," Muhammad said, picking up the W.B.A. belt, "I'm going to present this to George." Then he stopped for a moment. "Hmm. On second thought, I'm gonna keep it." They were still laughing as I marched over to pick up the belt. Biding my time, I sat down again. *I'll get him at the next joke.* My chance came a minute later. I sneaked behind him, put one hand on each side of the vent of his expensively elegant jacket, and ripped upward.

Muhammad went berserk. Contorting his face into an angry mask, he grabbed me but didn't swing. I'd grown up with guys who'd knock your head off if you messed with them that way. Of course, that was instinct, this was theater. "You Christian!" he screamed. "You blankety-blank!" *Christian? What does he mean that I'm an American?*

Trying to get his hands off of me, I was laughing, because evidently no one had seen me rip his coat. "What's wrong here?" everyone kept asking. "What happened?" Finally, three or four guys managed to pull him away. Still enraged, he continued spewing an endless stream of obscenities, then picked up some bottles off the dais and threatened to throw them.

Ali's reaction offered insights. I knew without doubt that he didn't like me, but now I saw through his game. Like Joe Frazier protesting that I shouldn't tell him to shut up, Ali's grabbing me—but not taking a swing—gave me an advantage. Also, I began disbelieving his religious commitment. I figured a man who swore so effortlessly and creatively wasn't exactly Godfearing, at least not in the way I understood or wanted to understand.

Later, still wondering why Ali had spit the word "Christian" at me like a curse, I recalled a meeting I'd had the previous year with representatives of Saudi Arabia about a possible deal to endorse Saudi sports.

"What do you hunt for there?" I'd asked.

The answer came through an interpreter. "Christians," he'd said. "We hunt for Christians." Then laughter.

So maybe that's what Muhammad Ali meant: Christians were animals, and the word "Christian" was a slur.

This was discouraging, because at the time I'd been giving Islam serious thought, sort of trying it on for size. In fact, as far back as 1969, *Muhammad Speaks*, the newspaper published by the Nation of Islam, had influenced me to stop eating pork. If I discovered that someone in my kitchen had cooked bacon or ham or pork ribs, I'd throw out all the pans and utensils and buy new ones.

There was something appealing about what the Nation's polite, clean-cut, self-disciplined young men in suits and bow ties represented. And while I wasn't completely ready to adopt their ways, in this time of great emptiness I'd inched closer toward becoming a Muslim—until Ali's poor manners ended my flirtation. I figured if a religion couldn't make you into a better person, it had no purpose at all, and if his was the true face of Islam, I didn't want to see it in my mirror.

Naturally, this didn't end my search for something, anything, to fill the emptiness. Around the same time I became infatuated with the television show *Kung Fu*, which starred David Carradine as a priest from an ancient order of Buddhist martial artists. Each episode contained nuggets of philosophy, sandwiched between the action sequences, that seemed to stick in my mind. *Now this is something I can relate to.* I wondered whether I might be able to learn that religion and become as wise as David Carradine appeared to be—until I saw him and his wife interviewed by Dick Cavett and she breast-fed their infant on camera. *Never mind.*

Before the Ali fight, scheduled for October 1974, in Kinshasa, Zaire, reporters from every major publication in the country—and outside it—came to interview me at my ranch in Livermore, California. One of them was my old hero Jim Brown, on assignment from ABC, the network that would broadcast the event from Africa. I took him on a complete tour—swimming pools, horses, houses, and guest houses. When the cameras stopped rolling and we were alone he said, "Man, George, you've really got it together. I'm going to get it together like you one day."

Like me? Jim Brown's going to get it together like *me*?

I was awestruck. He didn't know what he was talking about. This was Number 32, who'd starred in the first football game I'd ever watched on television, bulling his way over people and pulling five or six of them into the end zone. I hadn't even known who he was then. But I knew I wanted to walk like him. And I wanted my shoulders to be broad like his. And then when he took off the helmet, I saw the face that I wanted to wear. For me Jim Brown had ranked up there with Roy Rogers and John Wayne and *The Rifleman*, Chuck Connors. As a boy, I would close my eyes and pretend to be them. And now one of them was saying that I had it together and he didn't. The world had turned upside down.

Still looking for answers, I took a Bible to Zaire. It had been given to me some months before, when I'd visited a church that was supposed to have a lot of "nice, pretty girls" in the congregation. Nice was the operative word, since pretty girls were constantly throwing themselves at me; some even offered me money. "Is there anyone new to our church who would like to join?" the preacher had asked. To make the proper impression, I'd raised my hand and mounted the dais. Afterward, the preacher had handed me a new Good Book. "Here, George," he said. "In case you ever run into trouble, this will be your strength." I'd never looked at it, but I took it to Zaire. Embarrassed by it, however—feeling that if I was going to cling on to religion that it ought to be an African religion—I hid my Bible from view.

Still, I knew it was there in my room, my good luck charm. I even uttered a prayer now and then: "God, help me to get this knockout." But I guess He had other plans.

I was miserable in Zaire, not least because of the food. Tyree Lyons, my cook who'd worked at the Job Corps site in Pleasanton, scoured Kinshasa for edible chow (he eventually came down with some mysterious ailment that swelled his hands and eyes) and found little. But I hated more than the absence of cheeseburgers. My first quarters were an old army base infested with rats, lizards, and insects. Surrounded by cyclone fencing and barbed wire, it was patrolled and inhabited by rowdy soldiers who drank a lot more beer than I like to see in people toting loaded rifles. Finally I found a suite at the Intercontinental Hotel. Worried about someone coming in and messing with me and my things, I hired guards to keep a twenty-four-hour watch outside the room. This was clearly Muhammad Ali country. Sentiment in his favor colored how everyone looked at me—and they did so incessantly, their eyes following me everywhere. Most people wanted him to win back the title as much as he did. As far as he was concerned, he said, George Foreman held the championship taken from him for refusing to register for the military draft. And who was I? The goof who'd waved the American flag. I realized that no matter what happened in the ring, I couldn't win for losing. If I knocked him out, the most I'd get would be grudging respect for vanquishing a legend. And if I lost, there'd be a big crowd at the station, jeering me back to Palookaville.

Two weeks after my arrival in Zaire, and five days before the fight, I was cut over the eye during a sparring session; I had walked into an elbow my partner raised to protect himself from my savagery. Blood spurted. "Hey, I'm cut," I yelled.

"No, you're not," Sadler said. "You're all right."

"Stop everything," I insisted. "I'm cut."

That raised a flag in me. The trainer's job is to protect his fighter. Many's the time less serious finger cuts have caused lengthy postponements, for the simple reason that a championship contest is intended to be a match between both men at their best. Distrusting local doctors, I had Sadler place a butterfly adhesive over the cut in anticipation of flying to Belgium or France for proper medical treatment and regrouping. But, fearing that I wouldn't return, Zaire president Mobutu Sese Seko, who had cut the deal with Don King to sponsor the fight, refused to let me leave until after the bout, which he intended to be a showcase for his country. The month's postponement we did get wasn't nearly long enough for me to heal properly and begin the training cycle again, since the doctors forbade me from sweating for a minimum of ten days. No sweating, obviously, means no sparring or road work.

Like the lazy fox who couldn't reach the grapes, I convinced myself that I didn't need sparring and road work anyway; knocking out Muhammad Ali was a mere formality. Despite his crowing, I still believed he was afraid. I remembered the fear in his eye when I beat Ken Norton. He'd tried to cover with bravado, but having grown up with that stuff, I could spot it across the street. His not swinging at me when I tore his coat meant there was no reason to psych him out further. Yeah, he was scared. I saw it again when I ran into him and his friends at a Kinshasa nightspot.

I thought we were covered. Dick Sadler came to me for $25,000 to slip the referee under the table. I asked why. "Because," he said, "you've got a habit of hitting people when they're down, man. I want to make sure he doesn't disqualify you." I gave him the money, because that's how the game was played. Whether Zack Clayton ever received it, I don't know.

As usual before fighting, I was thirsty. Years before, Sadler had insisted that I dry out before the weigh-in and fight. Hungry to learn and determined to do what's right, I didn't question the wisdom, even though heavyweights aren't disallowed for tipping the scales. One time after a weigh-in I ate the usual poached eggs and toast breakfast with Charley Shipes, who was also on that evening's card. Man, he must not want to win, I thought when he drank glass after glass of water. I figured drying out was some secret Sadler weapon to build strength, the way marathon runners would later load up on carbohydrates before a race. Since Sadler had trained or worked with other heavyweight champs, I also figured he must know something.

"Ready for your glass of water?" he'd always ask in the dressing room just before the fight.

"Yeah, give it to me."

"Okay, take a nice drink."

I'd swallow the contents in two big, refreshing gulps.

"How was that?"

"Great."

"Okay, good. Now here's a couple pieces of ice."

A treat.

The feeling of near dehydration, relieved only partially by the short drink and ice chips, contributed to an overall mood Sadler created. I was thirsty, in more ways than one. He'd wind me up with curse after vicious curse, describing the destruction of that evil blankety-blank waiting in the ring. By the time he turned me loose, I'd become an exploding monster. The result: forty fights and forty victories, thirty-seven of them by knockout, most in the early rounds. Why question success?

At four o'clock in the morning, on October 30, 1974, I awaited my fate in the locker room. Later I would read that Muhammad Ali's arrival in the ring was greeted by tribal drumbeats and a crowd roaring "Al-ee, Al-ee." But I was aware of none of that. My thoughts were elsewhere. I wanted to end the fight, collect my money, and get home. Who'd ever fought at four A.M.? But it wasn't four in the morning where it counted: back home. There it was prime time. And we were live via satellite, the focus of the world's attention.

"Are you ready for your water now?" Sadler asked. We'd kept Muhammad waiting in the ring long enough.

"Yep," I said. Just like always.

I took a big swallow and almost spit it back into the cup.

"Man," I said, "this tastes like medicine. This water have medicine in it?"

"SAME WATER AS ALWAYS," he yelled.

"All right," I said. I drank the rest, which tasted just as medicinal.

With the aftertaste on my tongue, I climbed into the ring accompanied by tepid cheers and scattered boos. I looked over at

Muhammad in his corner, clowning around. When he wouldn't return my stare, I knew for sure that he was afraid of me.

Muhammad's introduction by the ring announcer brought an ecstatic ovation. He was incredibly popular, maybe even more popular than their president, Mobutu. Muhammad Ali was their man. In fact, Muhammad Ali was everyone's man. Everywhere he fought, his opponents faced the same disadvantage I did, receiving polite applause that seemed even more sparse in contrast.

While referee Zack Clayton gave us the instructions, Muhammad finally looked me in the eye. We glared at each other. My only thought was to knock him out early.

At the opening bell, Muhammad became a rabbit. He'd flick a jab at me and run. Me, I rushed him like a tiger, throwing hard shot after hard shot, going for that early shower. But he was one tough rabbit to catch, even for a tiger. Somehow, we always ended up on the ropes or in the corner, with me whaling away and him covering up. I'd jab, jab, jab, then throw several knockout punches that couldn't find their mark. He'd hold on to me, and the ref would break us apart. Still, though, he'd hold on, pressing his elbows against my back as I bent over.

His only offense was that famous flicking jab. It came so fast, you could barely see it, let alone counter it. Each time he threw one, I'd think, *Man, that's a quick jab.* I soon figured out that he was trying to open the cut over my eye. But I wasn't worried. Any minute, I knew, he was going down, just as every other opponent of mine had.

For the first two rounds I unleashed a torrent of punches, none of which really found its mark. Muhammad was a master at covering up. Not until the third round did I land a solid blow. It was a wicked right hand that struck home just under his heart. Blows like that can drive the wind—and the will—out of a man. Muhammad looked at me as if to say, "Hey, I'm not going to take that off you." That made me happy, because I thought then that he'd finally stand toe to toe with me, his pride getting the better of his intelligence. No way could he win a slugging match with me; we both knew that. But when I charged after him, his intelligence prevailed. He backed into the ropes and began covering up to avoid another barrage of heavy shots. I beat on him mercilessly, trying to connect with one of those home-run punches.

At the sound of the bell ending the round, Muhammad's face looked like he'd just seen a miracle. He had: his own survival—he was still on his feet.

Back in my corner, Sadler and Archie Moore insisted that I keep up the pounding. But I was already nearly exhausted. I couldn't understand why. I'd fought only three rounds, yet felt that I'd gone fifteen.

In the next round, we continued playing predator and prey. He'd hit me with one shot—usually the jab, but sometimes a right—then run. He had to, because when he faced me I placed my left foot between both of his feet. That meant his alternatives were to either stand in front of me and fight or move backward. So of course he moved backward and covered up. He was helped by an apparently loose top rope, which allowed him to lean way out of the ring, his head beyond my reach. No one in my camp had checked the ropes before the fight. Why bother? For years now, my fight plan had been to take off my robe, get a quick knockout, put the robe back on, and return to the dressing room. Who worried about the tautness or slackness of the ropes? Now Muhammad was the beneficiary of that lack of attention to detail.

In that fourth round I was able finally to land a thundering right on the back of his neck. It weakened him, and I knew that if I could land another one like that, he'd go down and out. But when I loaded up the weapon and cocked it, I saw something that made me pull back instead. That sight is, in fact, the image I recall most vividly from the fight. It was the face of a "friend," sitting at ringside, who happened to be directly in my line of vision. (What he did bothered me so much that I've put him out of my mind forever; I can't even remember his name.) Between when I threw the first shot and prepared to throw the second, he began waving his arms wildly and screaming, "Bull! He hit him behind the neck. He's cheating." A man I'd considered family was rooting against me. In a state of shock, I couldn't deliver the punch that probably would have ended the fight right there. For the rest of the night I wondered whether he'd do the same thing every time I threw one.

My hurt and disappointment, and that thinking, lessened whatever power I had left. And there wasn't much of it. I wondered what had happened to my stamina, let alone my strength. No matter what the sports writers said, stamina was never one of my problems; I'd had plenty of it. But because they'd not seen it—with my fights usually ending in the early rounds—they'd assumed I lacked it. I guess they hadn't noticed that I'd gone the distance three times before, and had even once scored a tenth-round knockout (of Gregorio Peralta).

It seemed that this was turning into a déjà vu nightmare of my amateur fights against Clay Hodges. Man, was I tired. I could barely get off the stool between rounds. Even so, Sadler was instructing me to continue my fearsome attack. This contradicted his usual advice, which was to slowly and carefully build to the knockout. "Get him," he said. "He can't last another round."

Archie Moore wasn't as insistent as Sadler; at least, he didn't say as much. This man of great pride had been disturbed and hurt, I think, by my pushing him to the side in favor of Sadler again. If either guy had told me to change tactics, I would have. They could have said to back off a round or two, catch my breath, and let him come to me; he'd have to, if he wanted to win, because by then he was far behind on points. But because these guys counseled me to attack, attack, attack, I did. Their job was to give advice. Mine was to take it.

Every time I went to hit Muhammad, he'd cover up, strike me with that one quick jab or right, then run. The sad part was that my blows, which numbered at least five to one over his, were met by the crowd with either silence or, worse, the reaction of my "friend." Meanwhile, each one of Muhammad's little jabs brought tumultuous cries. I was winning these rounds, but Muhammad Ali owned their hearts and minds more completely with every punch he absorbed. For them, this had become a morality play: Muhammad was good and I was evil. And yet, it was because of me, as champion, that this fight had been staged in Zaire. George Foreman, not Muhammad Ali, had tried to do something grand for Africa, had brought the television cameras to show off Africa to the world, had made the Africans proud of themselves. I'd wanted them to love me, too—and for some reason they didn't. I vowed never to go back.

In the seventh round, Muhammad noticed that I was getting tired, that my shots weren't hurting as much. He said, "Come on, George, show me something. Is that all you got?"

Knowing that he was whistling in the graveyard, I figured, *Okay, I'm just going to play around now, catch him talking, and let him try to hit me. When he tries, I'll knock him out.* As tired and weak as I felt, I always believed that I still had enough for that one shot to end it all. All I needed was the chance, the opening. If Muhammad made the mistake of coming to me, it would be his last mistake that night.

Angelo Dundee, Muhammad's trainer, must have divined my plan. He yelled out, "Don't play with the sucker, don't play." A few years before, he'd been present at a fight of mine in Lake Geneva, Wisconsin, and had seen the ferocious beating I'd given a tough Jamaican boxer. So he understood the damage I could do.

Angelo's warning seemed to sober Muhammad a little. He stopped playing around and talking.

In the eighth, I tried to entice Muhammad to come to me. Dropping my hands, I followed him around the ring, as if daring him to step into my web; there was no way he could hurt me. When we neared the ropes, I began pummeling him again. He was knocked backward near the corner, then bounced to the side. Off balance, I turned to follow him and was leaning his way when he threw a left-right combination whose power was multiplied by both my leaning toward him as I tried to re-balance myself, and his momentum off the corner.

As the combination struck ground zero on my chin, I remember thinking, *Boy, I'm going down.* Muhammad, I'm sure, was as surprised as I was.

My fall to the mat felt that much harder because my legs had been twisted while I was off balance. On my back, I lifted my head and not only was I alert and uninjured, I was actually excited and hopeful: *This guy hasn't mixed it up with me all night. Now, when he thinks he can come in and finish the job, I'll be able to get him. It doesn't matter how tired I am—I've still got enough to put him down when I get the chance. And now I will.*

Though I could have, I didn't get up immediately. Because in the days when there were no standing eight-counts that would allow a boxer to clear his senses before reentering the fray, the custom developed to stay down until eight. Instead of watching the referee's count, you were supposed to look for your cornermen's signal. Even as I did, I could hear Zack Clayton's count. He said "eight" and Sadler motioned me up. I stood at once, but Clayton waved me off with a quick count—nine and ten became one word to me.

It was over.

Clayton guided me to my corner as Ali and the crowd began celebrating. My God, it was over. It was really over. I felt disappointed, less for losing than for not getting a chance to mix it up. Then the magnitude of the loss began to hit me. I would be sorting it out for a long time.

"All right?" Sadler asked.

"Yeah."

Back in the dressing room, the mood was funereal. While dejection had set in, I was still more tired than anything else. Lying there on the training table, letting the thoughts just come and go, I heard questions—impertinent questions—from sportswriters they wouldn't have dared to ask even twenty-four hours before. Now these guys believed they could get away with anything. *So that's how it is? You're either on top, or you're nowhere.*

In short order, I would become depressed beyond recognition, and this fight would go down in boxing history; no less than Norman Mailer wrote an entire book about it.

Muhammad began bragging about his great strategy—letting me punch myself out before delivering the crowning blows. But I know, and he knows, he had no such strategy before the fight. To say he did is to shoot an arrow into a barn and then paint a bull's-eye around it. Muhammad's only strategy had been survival. When I cut off the ring from him, he had nowhere to go but the ropes, and nothing to do but cover up. What's more true than his concoction of some brilliant strategy is that I fought a foolish fight by not letting him come to me more, especially when I was tired and far ahead on points. I hadn't done that because I couldn't let anyone think that George Foreman was afraid of Muhammad Ali, and because my trainers told me to give it my all.

"Rope-a-dope" the fight got nicknamed when I mentioned to a writer that I believed my water may have been mickeyed. What else, I asked, could account for that medicinal taste and my terrible tiredness? What else could account for how sick and sore I felt for a month afterward?

So was there "medicine" in my drink? I can't say for certain. Later, I heard that Sugar Ray Robinson, watching the fight at home in the States, had commented to a friend that I seemed drugged. Maybe sportswriter Jim Murray, aiming for a laugh, was closer to the mark than he realized when he wrote that I looked like "a drunk trying to find a keyhole."

If I had been slipped a mickey, why? I can't answer with certainty there, either. Only afterward, when I thought about Sadler and my relationship with him, did it seem somewhat plausible. I remembered some stories he used to tell about boxers who belonged to gangsters—how the fix would be in for this guy or that to lose in order to set up a bigger payday or better betting odds down the line.

Such stories poured out of him when we were on the road and bored. We laughed about them. I was young and considered Sadler a father figure. Was he joking? I don't know. But surely his message between the lines was that he'd protect me from such nastiness.

There was the tale Sadler told of an aging heavyweight who threw a fight to an up-and-coming champ. After the third round, the trainer put the stool out for his aging heavyweight, who angrily kicked it over backward. That told the trainer that his fighter was going down. A man who's soon to hit the canvas doesn't need the rest.

"I felt so bad," the trainer said. I thought he felt bad because he believed his man had thrown the fight. Then he clarified: "He could've at least given *me* a chance to make some money on it too."

The years since the fight have not answered the question for me of whether I was indeed doped. One verifiable fact is that Muhammad had been the heavy underdog until a late flurry brought down the odds. Was that money bet with the heart? I know only that this fight featured more unexplained happenings than any event of my life, and that in the grand scheme of things the loss ultimately helped to make me a man. Back then, however, I believed that the sky had fallen. I wasn't champion anymore. I didn't know what I was.

As for that Bible I'd taken to Zaire, the one given me by the preacher: I put it away where I wouldn't see it anymore. What good was a Bible if it didn't bring you luck?

~

[FIFTEEN]

Ali vs. Frazier III: "The Thrilla in Manila"

By Lance Pugmire

Frazier had won the first match; Ali the second. This third fight in the Philippines would be the rubber match. Frazier was motivated to win back the title he had lost to Foreman. And Ali wanted to show that he was still The Greatest. Lance Pugmire is boxing beat reporter for the Los Angeles Times. —K.M.

The bright morning sun typically symbolizes the birth of a new day, the start of something potentially magnificent.

In October 1975, after Muhammad Ali closed his historic trilogy with Joe Frazier in a superior battle that some rank as boxing's ultimate prizefight, co-promoter Bob Arum recalls exiting the Araneta Coliseum to burning heat.

"Like something had died," Arum said.

The best of Ali and Frazier came out during third and final meeting, the "Thrilla in Manila."

Frazier won their first meeting in 1971, a bout between two unbeatens that is considered one of the greatest spectacles of the sports century. Ali won the rematch in 1974.

Frazier's disdain for Ali rose before the third meeting, with the champion boasting their fight in the Philippines would be a "killa and a thrilla and a chilla when I get that gorilla in Manila."

President Ferdinand Marcos struck a deal with promoter Don King to bring the bout across the Pacific.

"Ali is a promoter's dream. He created the magic of excitement," King said. "Frazier took (the gorilla comment) to heart, though, never really forgave him for that."

He should have, King said, pointing to Ali's attention to human rights that included his previous conscientious-objector stand against the Vietnam War.

"Ali stood for something," King said. "He stood up for the African American. It was about being a man, m–a–n.

"Look, no one will ever be able to say how great Ali was because he lost four years at the peak of his career standing up for a cause (objecting to the Vietnam War), for humanity and the unalienable rights of life, liberty and the pursuit of happiness that he felt would be denied him. Muhammad Ali stood for America."

The bout was staged in the Philippines, King said, because Marcos pushed to stage a symbolic battle between two proven boxing warriors who could bring attention to the past obscured war efforts of Filipinos in the battlegrounds of Iwo Jima, Okinawa and Saipan.

"This fight was about manhood," King said. "The rubber match ,.. was super sensational. It will be immortalized for the standard of time. Ali said it was the closest to death he's ever been.

"The fight illustrated man's courage, the spirit that nobody can fight your battle but you, and the enemy is in front of you. They had that will of giving it their all, for all mankind."

Ali, the champion at that time following his epic "Rumble in the Jungle" victory a year earlier over George Foreman, ruled the first four rounds, belting Frazier with precise blows.

Frazier rallied impressively, dominating with power left-handed shots and his patented toughness that continually gave Ali fits.

"I hit him with punches that'd bring down the walls of a city," Frazier said afterward.

Both men were gassed in the late championship rounds. Ali scored hurtful blows on Frazier, swelling the former champion's eyes and blasting him with hard rights to the head in the 14th round that might have impaired or killed—a less fit, weaker foe.

After 14 rounds, Frazier's trainer Eddie Futch concluded that his fighter, with bad left-eye vision and a swollen right eye, couldn't see anymore.

In the opposite corner, an exhausted Ali, comfortably ahead on scorecards that differed from those kept in ringside reporters' notebooks, had cornerman Angelo Dundee urging him on for three more minutes.

"Ali was going to give his life. He had to perform," King said. "I remember it like it was yesterday. Ali told me it was the closest to death he had ever came, but that the cause was more worthy than he. The cause of manhood.

"That fight was the epitome, showing man's incredible will to withstand the withering battle of blow after blow. After a fight like that, there was no way you could be the fighter that you were."

Futch dramatically decided Frazier had had enough, waving the towel, stopping the fight against Frasier's objections.

"It wasn't Joe Frazier who stopped the fight," King said. "It was Eddie Futch. He stopped his fighter from being hurt any worse, physically and psychologically. God bless Eddie Futch."

Years later, an aged Frazier was shown hitting a heavy bag in an HBO documentary about the Thrilla in Manila, suggesting he'd gotten the best of Ali in the end, because his punishment contributed to Ali's being ravaged by Parkinson's.

King recalls a more uplifting review of the clash.

"It was so wonderful for Muhammad because (of) when they were making him the bad guy years earlier about not going to fight the Viet Cong . . . People were finally able to see after this test of manhood that he was truly fighting for freedom of religion, against the system that allowed the horrific, barbaric things that were being done to our people," King said.

"He is the people's hero. For black and white. He always told me, 'Never let 'em down.'"

~

"Ali's 'Thrilla in Manila' stands the test of time," Lance Pugmire, June 4, 2016, Licensed by Los Angeles Times.

[SIXTEEN]

My Dinner with Ali

By Davis Miller

Ali had 10 more professional bouts after the Thrilla in Manila. He remained world champion until 1978 when he lost the belt to Leon Spinks, then won it back a few months later in a rematch. Ali fought his last fight in 1981 before hanging up his gloves for good. Two years later he is diagnosed with Parkinson's disease. One spring day in 1988, Davis Miller drops by on Ali in Louisville and spends a remarkable evening with the champ. Republished here, his story "My Dinner with Ali" was previously anthologized in The Best American Sports Writing of the Century. —K.M.

~

One

March 31, 1988

I'd been waiting for years. When it finally happened, it wasn't what I'd expected. But he's been fooling many of us for most of our lives.

When I finally got to see him, it wasn't at his farm in Michigan and I didn't have an appointment. I simply drove past his mother's house on Lambert Avenue in Louisville.

It was midafternoon on Good Friday, two days before Resurrection Day. A block-long ivory-colored Winnebago with Virginia plates was parked out front. Though he hadn't been in town much lately, I knew it was his.

How was I sure? Because I knew his patterns and style. Since 1962, when he has traveled unhurried in this country, he's preferred buses or recreational vehicles. And he owned a second farm in Virginia. The connections were obvious. Some people study faults in the earth's crust or the habits of storms or of galaxies, hoping to make sense of the universe, of the world we live in, and of their own lives. Others meditate on the life and work of one social movement or man. Since I was eleven years old, I have been a Muhammad Ali scholar.

I parked my car behind his Winnebago and grabbed a few old magazines and a special stack of papers I'd been storing under the front seat, waiting for the meeting with Ali that, ever since my family and I'd moved to Louisville two years before, I'd been certain would come. Like everyone else, I wondered in what shape I'd find The Champ. I'd heard about his Parkinson's disease and watched him stumble through the ropes when introduced at recent big fights. But when I thought of Ali, I remembered him as I'd seen him years before, when he was luminous.

I was in my early twenties then, hoping to become a world-champion kickboxer. And I was fortunate enough to get to spar with him. I later wrote a couple of stories about the experience, the ones I had with me today hoping that he'd sign.

Yes, in those days he had shone. There was an aura of light and confidence around him. He had told the world of his importance: "I am the center of the universe," he howled throughout the mid-1970s, and we almost believed him. But recent magazine and newspaper articles had Ali sounding like a turtle spilled on to his back, limbs thrashing air.

It was his brother Rahaman who opened the door. He saw what I was holding under my arm, smiled an understanding smile, and said, "He's out in the Winnebago. Go knock on the door. He'll be happy to sign those for you."

Rahaman looked pretty much the way I remembered him: tall as his brother, mahogany skin, and a mustache that suggested a cross between footballer Jim Brown and a black, aging Errol Flynn. There was no indication in his voice or on his face that I would find his brother less than healthy.

I crossed the yard, climbed the three steps on the side of the Winnebago, and prepared to knock. Ali opened the door before I got the chance. I'd forgotten how huge he was. His presence filled the doorway. He had to lean under the frame to see me.

I felt no nervousness. Ali's face, in many ways, was as familiar to me as my father's. His skin remained unmarked, his countenance had nearly perfect symmetry. Yet something was different: Ali was no longer the world's prettiest man. This was only partly related to his illness; it was also because he was heavier than he needed to be. He remained handsome, even uncommonly so, but in the way of a youngish granddad who tells stories about how he could have been a movie star, if he'd wanted. Ali's pulchritude used to challenge us; now he looked a bit more like us, and less like an avatar sent by Allah.

"Come on in," he said and waved me past. His voice had a gurgle to it, as if he needed to clear his throat. He offered a massive hand. He did not so much shake hands as he lightly placed his in mine. His touch was as gentle as a girl's. His palm was cool and not callused; his fingers were the long, tapered digits of a hypnotist; his fingernails were professionally manicured; his knuckles were large and slightly swollen, as if he recently had been punching the heavy bag.

He was dressed in white, all white: new leather tennis shoes, over-the-calf cotton socks, custom-tailored linen slacks, thick short-sleeved safari-style shirt crisp with starch. I told him I thought white was a better color for him than the black he often wore those days.

He motioned for me to sit, but didn't speak. His mouth was tense at the corners; it looked like a kid's who has been forced by a parent or teacher to keep it closed. He slowly lowered himself into a chair beside the window. I took a seat across from him and laid my magazines on the table between us. He immediately picked them up, produced a pen, and began signing. He asked, "What's your name?" and I told him.

He continued to write without looking up. His eyes were not glazed, as I'd read, but they looked tired. A wet cough rattled in his throat. His left hand trembled almost continuously. In the silence around us, I felt a need to tell him some of the things I'd been wanting to say for years.

"Champ, you changed my life," I said. Its true. "When I was a kid, I was messed up, couldn't even talk to people. No kind of life at all." He raised his eyes from an old healthy image of himself on a magazine cover. "You made me believe I could do anything," I said.

He was watching me while I talked, not judging, just watching. I picked up a magazine from the stack in front of him. "This is a story I wrote for *Sports Illustrated* when I was in college," I said. "Its about the ways you've influenced my life."

"What's your name?" he asked again, this time looking right at me.

I told him. He nodded. I'll finish signing these in a while," he said. He put his pen on the table. "Read me your story."

"You have a good face," he said when I was through. "I like your face. Kind."

He'd listened seriously as I'd read, laughing at funny lines and when I'd tried to imitate his voice. He had not looked bored. It was a lot more than I could have expected.

"You ever seen any magic?" he asked. "You like magic?"

"Not in years," I said.

He stood and walked to the back of his RV, moving mechanically.

It was my great-grandfather's walk. He motioned for me to follow. There was a sad yet lovely, noble, and intimate quality to his movements.

He did about ten tricks. The one that interested me most required no props. It was a very simple deception. "Watch my feet," he said, standing maybe eight feet away, his back to me and his arms perpendicular to his sides. Then, although he'd just had real trouble walking, he seemed to levitate about three inches off of the floor. He turned to me and in his thick, slow voice said, "I'm a *baadd* niggah," and gave me the classic easy Ali smile.

I laughed and asked him to do it again; it was a good one. I thought I might like to try it myself, just as fifteen years earlier I had stood in front of the mirror in my dad s hallway for hours, pushing my tapeworm of a left arm out at the reflection, wishing mightily that I could replicate Ali s cobra jab. And I had found an old white cotton laundry bag, filled it with socks and rags, and hung it from a ceiling beam in the basement. I pulled on a pair of my dad's old brown cotton work gloves and pushed my left hand into that twenty-pound marshmallow two hundred, three hundred, five hundred, one thousand times a day—concentrating on speed: dazzling, crackling speed, in pursuit of godly speed, trying to whip out punches so fast they'd be invisible to opponents. I got to where I could shoot six to eight crisp shots a second—"shoe shinin'," Ali called it—and I strove to make my fists move more quickly than thought (like Ali's); and then I'd try to spring up on my toes, as I had watched Ali do: I would try to fly like Ali, bounding away from the bag and to my left.

After the levitation trick, Ali grabbed an empty plastic milk jug from beside a sink. He asked me to examine it. "What if I make this jug rise up from the sink this high and sit there? Will you believe?"

"Not much of a believer these days, Champ," I said.

"Well, what if I make it rise, sit this high off the ground, then turn in a circle?"

"I'm a hard man to convince," I said.

"Well, what if I make it rise, float over here to the other side of the room, then go back to the sink, and sit itself back down. Then will you become . . . one of my believers?"

I laughed and said, "Then I'll believe."

"Watch," he said, pointing at the plastic container and taking four steps back. I was trying to see both the milk jug and Ali. He waved his hands a couple of times in front of his body, said, "Arise, ghost, arise," in a foggy-sounding voice. The plastic container did not move from the counter.

"April Fool's," said Ali. We both chuckled and he walked over and slipped his long arm around my shoulders.

He autographed the stories and wrote a note on a page of my book-length manuscript I'd asked him to take a look at. "To Davis Miller, The Greatest Fan of All Times," he wrote. "From Muhammad Ali, King of Boxing."

I felt my stories were finally complete, now that he'd confirmed their existence. He handed me the magazines and asked me into his mother's house. We left the Winnebago. I unlocked my car and leaned across the front seat, carefully placing the magazines and manuscript on the passenger's side, not wanting to take a chance of damaging them or leaving them behind. Abruptly, there was a chirping, insect-sounding noise in my ear. I jumped back, swatted the air, turned around. It had been Ali's hand. He was standing right behind me, still the practical joker.

"How'd you do that?" I wanted to know. It was a question I'd find myself asking several times that day.

He didn't answer. Instead, he raised both fists to shoulder height and motioned me out into the yard. We walked about five paces, I put up my hands, and he tossed a slow jab at me. I blocked and countered with my own. Many fighters throw punches at each other or at the air or at whatever happens to be around. It's the way we play, even decades after having last stepped between the ropes of a prize ring. Now, approaching ten years after his retirement, Ali must still have tossed a hundred lefts a day. He and I had both thrown our shots a full half foot away from the other, but my adrenal gland was pumping at high gear from being around Ali and my jab had come out fast—it had made the air sing. He slid back a half step and took a serious look at me. I figured I was going to get it now. A couple of kids were riding past on bicycles; they recognized Ali and stopped.

"He doesn't understand I'm the greatest boxer of all times," he yelled to the kids. He pulled his watch from his arm, stuck it in his pants pocket. I slipped mine off, too. He'd get down to business now. He got up on his skates, danced to his left a little, loosening his legs. A couple of minutes before, climbing down the steps of his RV, he'd moved so awkwardly he'd almost lost his balance. I'd wanted to give him a hand, but knew not to. I'd remembered seeing old Joe Louis "escorted" in that fashion by lesser mortals, and I couldn't do that to Muhammad Ali. But now that Ali was on his toes and boxing, he was moving fairly fluidly.

He flung another jab in my direction, a second, a third. He wasn't one-fourth as fast as he had been in 1975, when I'd sparred with him, but his eyes were alert, shining like black electric marbles, and he saw everything and was real relaxed. That's one reason old fighters keep making comebacks: we are more alive when boxing than at almost any other time. The grass around us was green and was getting high; it would soon need its first cutting. A blue jay squawked from a big oak to the left. Six robins roamed the yard. The afternoon light was tawny. New leaves looked wet with the sun. I instinctively blocked and/or slid to the side of all three of Ali s punches, then immediately felt guilty about it, like being fourteen years old and knowing for the first time that you can beat your dad at ping-pong. I wished I could've stopped myself from slipping Ali's jabs, but I couldn't. Reflexive training runs faster and deeper than thought. I zipped a jab to his nose, one to his body, vaulted a straight right up to his chin, and was dead certain all three would have scored—and scored clean. A couple of cars stopped in front of the house. His mom's was on a corner lot. Three more were parked on the side.

"Check out the left," a young-sounding voice said from somewhere. The owner of the voice was talking about my jab, not Ali's.

"He's in with the triple greatest of all times," Ali was shouting.

"Gowna let him tire himself out. He'll get tired soon."

I didn't, but pretended to, anyway. "You're right, Champ," I told him, dropping my hands to my sides. "I'm thirty-five. Can't go like I used to."

I raised my right hand to my chest, acting out of breath. I looked at Ali; his hand was in the exact same position. We were both smiling, but he was sizing me up.

"He got scared," Ali shouted, conclusively.

Onlookers laughed from their bicycles and car windows. Someone blew his horn and another yelled, "Hey, Champ."

"Come on in the house," Ali said softly in my ear.

We walked toward the door, Ali in the lead, moving woodenly through new grass, while all around us people rolled up car windows and started their engines.

Two

"Gowna move back to Loovul, just part time."

The deep Southern melody rolled sleepily in Ali's voice. His words came scarcely louder than whisper and were followed by a short fit of coughing.

Back to Loovul. Back to hazy orange sunsets and ancestors' unmarked graves; back to old slow-walking family (real and acquired), empty sidewalks, nearly equatorial humidity, and to peach cobblers made by heavy, round-breasted aunts wearing flowered dresses; back to short thin uncles and their straw hats, white open-collared shirts, black shiny pants, and spit-shined black Florsheims—back to a life that hadn't been Ali's since he was eighteen years old.

We were standing in the "family room," a space so dark I could not imagine the drapes ever having been drawn, a room furnished with dented gold-painted furniture, filled with smells of cooking meat, and infused with a light not dissimilar to that from a fireplace fire.

Ali had introduced me to his mother, Mrs. Odessa Grady Clay, and to Rahaman, then suddenly he was gone.

Ali's family easily accepted me. They were not surprised to have a visitor and handled me with ritualistic charm and grace. Rahaman told me to make myself at home, offered a root beer, went to get it.

I took a seat on the sofa beside Ali's mother. Mrs. Clay was in her early seventies, yet her face had few wrinkles. Short, her hair nearly as orange as those Louisville sunsets, she was freckled, fragile-looking and pretty. Ali's face is shaped much like his mothers. During all the years he was fighting, she was quite heavy, but she had lost what looked to be about seventy-five pounds over the past ten years.

Mrs. Clay was watching Oprah Winfrey on a big old wooden floor-model TV. I was wondering where Ali had gone. Rahaman brought the drink, a paper napkin, and a coaster. Mrs. Clay patted me on the hand. "Don't worry," she said. "Ali hasn't left you. I'm sure he's just gone upstairs to say his prayers."

I hadn't realized that my anxiety was showing. But Ali's mother had watched him bring home puppies many times during his forty-six years. "He's always been a restless man, like his daddy," she said. "Can't ever sit still."

Mrs. Clay spoke carefully, with a mother's sweet sadness about her. The dignified clip to her voice must once have seemed affected, but after cometing all over the globe with Ali, it now sounded authentically old-money, poised-Kentuckian in its inflections.

"Have you met Lonnie, Ali's new wife?" she asked. "He's known her since she was a baby. I'm so happy for him. She's my best friend's daughter, we used to all travel to his fights together. She's a smart girl, has a master's degree in business. She's so good to him, doesn't use him. He told me, Mom, Lonnie's better to me than all the other three put together.' She treats him so good. He needs somebody to take care of him."

Just then, Ali came back to the room, carrying himself high and with stately dignity, though his footing was unsteady. He fell deep into a chair on the other side of the room.

"You tired, baby?" Mrs. Clay asked.

"Tired, I'm always tired," he said, rubbing his face twice and closing his eyes.

He must have felt me watching or was simply conscious of someone other than family being in the room. His eyes weren't closed ten seconds before he shook himself awake, balled his hands into fists, and started making typical Ali faces and noises at me—sticking his teeth out over his lower lip, looking fake-mean, growling, other playful cartoon kid stuff. After a few seconds he asked, "Y-y-you okay?" He was so difficult to understand that I didn't so much hear him as I conjectured what he must have been saying. "Y-y-you need anything? They takin' care of you?" I assured him that I was fine.

He made a loud clucking noise by pressing his tongue across the roof of his mouth and popping it forward. Rahaman came quickly from the kitchen. Ali motioned him close and whispered in his ear. Rahaman went back to the kitchen. Ali turned to me. "Come sit beside me," he said, patting a bar stool to his right. He waited for me to take my place, then said, "You had any dinner? Sit and eat with me."

"Can I use the phone? I need to call home and let my wife know."

"You got kids?" he asked. I told him I had two. He asked how old. I told him the ages.

"They know me?" he asked.

"Even the two-year-old. He throws punches at the TV whenever I play your fights."

He nodded, satisfied. "Bring 'em over Sunday," he said, matter-of-factly. "I'll do my magic for 'em. Here's my mother's number. Be sure to phone first."

I called Lyn and told her where I was and what I was doing. She didn't seem surprised. She asked me to pick up a gallon of milk on the way home. I was sure she was excited for me, but we had a lot of history, some of it rough, and she wouldn't show emotion in her voice simply because I was hanging out with my childhood idol. In September 1977, near the beginning of our first semester at East Carolina University, I packed my car with clothes for Lyn and me, picked her up from her noon art class, and drove straight to the bank, where we withdrew all of the money our parents had given us for the semester.

"Terry, sorry I'm not in class today," began the note I left on my writing teacher's office door. "I've taken my girlfriend to New York to see the Muhammad Ali—Earnie Shavers fight. Oh, were also going to get married while we're there. See you next week. Davis."

Lyn and I drove straight through the night, arriving in Manhattan the morning of the bout. Early afternoon, as we checked into a Howard Johnson's in New Jersey, Lyn put on the wedding band I'd purchased months before. We then drove from the motel back into the city, and, at a shop in the Waldorf-Astoria, she bought a simple jade ring for me. As we were leaving the hotel, we spotted Ali on the street. Traffic stopped in all directions. Thousands of us followed him as he walked to Madison Square Garden for the weigh-in. Even though there were several people near Ali who were taller and bigger than he, he looked larger than anyone I had seen in my life. There was a wakeful silence around him. As if his very skin was listening. There was pushing and shoving near the outside of the circle of people around Ali. Lyn and I stood on a concrete wall away from the clamor and looked down on him. There was a softness, a quietude, near the center of the circle; those closest to Ali were gentle and respectful.

That night in the Garden was the first time I'd seen twenty thousand people move as one organism. The air was alive with smells of pretzels and hot dogs, beer and marijuana. It was Ali's last good fight. Shavers's longtime ring nickname, "One Punch," had been arrived at because it took him exactly one good, clean, orgasmic overhand right to flatten opponents. Although few casual boxing fans had heard of Shavers, ring insiders regarded his right cross as the hardest of anyone's in the history of pugilism. Bigger than all of Foreman's punches. Bigger than Frazier's best left hook. Tonight, Ali was regularly hurt by Shavers's rights and would later say that Shavers had hit him harder than anyone ever. So resounding were the shots with which Shavers tagged Ali that Lyn and I heard them, the sound arriving what seemed a full second after we saw the punches connect, as we sat a quarter of a mile up and away from the ring. In round fifteen, we were all suddenly standing and not realizing that we had stood. I was trembling, Lyn was holding my hand, and thousands of us were chanting, "Ahh-lee, Ahh-lee," his name our mantra, as his gloves melded into vermilion lines of tracers and Shavers finally bowed before him.

The next morning, after watching Ali hold forth on the Today show and checking out of our motel, Lyn and I drove back to Manhattan to get a marriage license. That's when we discovered that there was a three-day waiting period. We had spent all but forty dollars of our money at the fight, on the motel, and on my wedding band. We could not afford to stay; she was very disappointed. Throughout our long drive back to eastern North Carolina, she stayed mostly silent and hung her head down toward her lap. When she'd started college, I'd known it was the first time she'd been away from her parents' house (the one and only home in which she'd lived) for longer than a weekend. What I hadn't recognized was how unformed she was, how young emotionally. Before the trip she'd seemed so tough; it surprised me that she depended on me even more than I on her. This was the first time she had seen me fail. To this day she's never gotten over it, a fact that initiated an ever-present darkening of our relationship. I was disappointed, too, but remained certain that she would soon cut loose, beyond the pull of gravity; she would become the ballsy, happier, primal-woods creature she really was inside.

The day we returned from New York she moved into my off-campus apartment, and for the rest of the year neither of us was able to find a job. We had to live off of what little money I was able to make modeling for art classes at the university. Even though I was certain everything would work out well, for Lyn it was a horrible time. I'd come in from classes and find her in tears, worrying about what her parents would do when they found out we'd blown their money and she was living with me. She eventually quit school because she had no funds to buy materials for her art classes. It would be nearly a year before we again felt we could afford to get married. Every weekend, to pay our electric bills, we filled a laundry bag (the same one I'd once used as a boxing bag) with returnable soda bottles we picked up beside highways. But, all these years later, I know that I'd be willing to do it the exact same way to see Ali in one of his last fights.

Now Rahaman brought two large bowls of chili and two enormously thick slices of white bread from the kitchen. Ali and I sat at our chairs, took spoons in our hands. He put his face down close to the bowl and the food was gone. Three minutes, tops. As I continued to eat, he spoke easily to me. "I remember what it was like to meet Joe Louis and Rocky Marciano for the first time," he said. "They were my idols. I'd seen their fights and faces so many times I felt I knew them. Want to treat you right, don't want to disappoint you.

"Do you know how many people in the world would like to have the opportunity you're getting, how many would like to come into my house and spend the day with me?" he said. "Haven't fought in seven years and still get over four hundred letters a week."

I asked how people got his address.

He looked puzzled. "I don't know," he answered, shaking his head. "Sometimes they come addressed 'Muhammad Ali, Los Angeles, California, USA.' Don't have a house in L.A. no more, but the letters still get to me.

"I want to get me a place, a coffee shop, where I can give away free coffee and doughnuts and people can just sit around and talk, people of all races, and I can go and talk to people. Have some of my old robes and trunks and gloves around, show old fight films, call it 'Ali's Place.'"

I'd call it 'Ali's'" I said, not believing there would or ever could be such a place but enjoying sharing his dream with him. "Just 'Ali's,' that's enough."

"'Ali's?" he repeated, and his eyes focused inward, visualizing the dream.

"People would know what it was," I said.

I asked if he had videotapes of his fights. He shook his head no.

"Well, look," I said, "I manage a video store."

"You're rich," he said, pointing and chuckling, but also being serious.

"No, no, I'm not. I just try to make a living. Look . . . why don't we go to the store and get a tape of your fights, and we can watch it tonight. Would you like that? You want to ride with me?"

"I'll drive," Ali said.

There was a rubber monster mask in the Winnebago that I wore on my hand on the way to the store, pressing it against the window at stoplights. A couple of times, people in cars saw the mask, then recognized Ali. Ali wore glasses when he read and when he drove. Every time that he saw someone looking at him, he carefully removed his glasses, placed them in his lap, made his hands into fists, and put them up beside his head.

Other than my alcoholic grandfather near the end of his life, Ali was the worst driver I'd ever ridden with. He careened from lane to lane, sometimes riding down the middle of the highway, and he often switched lanes without looking or giving turn signals. Still wearing the monster mask on my right hand, I balled my fists in my lap and pretended to be relaxed. A group of teenage boys became infuriated when he cut them off in their beat-up and rusted-out 1970s Firebird. Three of them leaned out the windows, shooting him the finger. Ali shot it back.

When we made it to the store, my co-workers acted as if they'd been stricken dumb. Instead of doing what they always did—talking about the day's business or problems they were having with customers or other employees, they stayed away and simply stared at Ali. We borrowed an early-1970s Godzilla movie Ali wanted to see and a tape of his fights and interviews called *Ali: Skill, Brains and Guts* that was written and directed by Jimmy Jacobs, the international handball champion and fight historian. Jacobs had recently died of a degenerative illness. Ali hadn't known of Jacobs's death until I told him.

"He was a good man," Ali said. His voice had that same quality that an older person's takes on who daily reads obituaries. "Did you know Bundini died?" he asked, speaking in the same tone he'd use with a friend of many years. I felt honored by his intimacy and told him that I'd heard.

In the Winnebago on the way back to his mom's, he said, "You're sincere. After thirty years, I can tell."

"I know a lot of people have tried to use you," I said.

"They have used me. But it don't matter. I don't let it change me."

I stopped by my car again on the way into Mrs. Clay's house. There was one more picture I hoped Ali would sign, but earlier I'd felt I might be imposing on him. It was a classic head shot in a beautiful out-of-print biography by Wilfrid Sheed that featured hundreds of wonderfully reproduced color plates. I grabbed the book from the car and followed Ali into the house.

When we were seated, I handed him the book and he signed the picture on the title page. "To Davis Miller, From Muhammad Ali, King of Boxing," he wrote, "3–31–88." And then, on the opposite page, which bore only his name in bold block lettering, he inscribed, "After me, there will never be another."

I was about to ask if he'd mind autographing the photo I especially wanted, but he turned to page three, signed that picture, then the next page and the next. He continued to sign for probably forty-five minutes, writing comments about opponents ("Get up Chump," he wrote beside the classic photo of the fallen Sonny Liston), parents, Elijah Muhammad ("The man who named me"), Howard Cosell ("Crazy"), spouses ("She gave me Hell," he scrawled across his first wife's picture; "Love is the net where Hearts are Caught like Fish," he carefully inscribed on a photo of him with his gleaming future wife, then seventeen-year-old Belinda Boyd, in her father's South Side Chicago bakery), then passed the book to his mother and brother to autograph a family portrait. He even signed "Cassius Clay" on several photos from the early sixties. He flipped twice through the book, autographing dozens and dozens of photos, pointing out annotations as he wrote.

"Never done this before," he said. "Usually sign one or two pictures."

As he turned from page to page, he stopped and studied, then autographed, a picture of his youthful self with the Louisville Sponsoring Group, the collective of rich white businessmen who owned his contract (and reputedly those of several race horses) until he became Muslim. He also hesitated over a famous posed shot taken for Life magazine in 1963, in a bank vault. In this photo, a wide-eyed and beaming Cassius Clay sits atop one million one-dollar bills. Ali turned to me and said, "Money don't mean nothin'," signed the picture with his childhood name, and leafed to a picture with Malcolm X, which he autographed, then posed his pen above the signature, as if prepared to make another annotation. Suddenly, though, he closed the book, looked at me dead level, and held it out at arms length with both hands. "I'm giving you somethin' very valuable," he said, handing me the biography as if deeding me the book of life.

Three

I excused myself to the bathroom, locking the door behind me. A pair of Ali's huge, shiny-black, businessman's dress shoes was on the floor beside the toilet. The toe of one had been crushed, the other was lying on its side. When I unlocked the door to leave, it wouldn't budge. I couldn't even turn the handle. After trying several times, I tentatively knocked. There was laughter from the other room. I distinctly heard Mrs. Clay and Rahaman murmuring. I yanked fairly hard on the door a few times. Nothing. Just when I was beginning to think I was stuck in Odessa Clays bathroom for the millennium, the door easily opened. I caught a glimpse of Ali bounding into a side room to the right, laughing and high-stepping like some oversized, out-of-shape Nubian leprechaun.

I peeked around the corner. He was standing with his back flat against the wall. He saw me, jumped from the room, and tickled me, a guilty-little-kid smile splashed across his features. Next thing I knew, he had me on the floor, balled up in a fetal position, tears flowing down both sides of my face, laughing. Then he stopped tickling me and helped me to my feet. Everybody kept laughing. Mrs. Clay's face was round and wide with laughter. One-fourth Irish, her ancestry traceable to the village of Ennis, County Clare, the former Odessa Grady looked like the mom of a Celtic imp.

"What'd you think happened to the door?" Rahaman asked. I told him I'd figured it was Ali. "Then why you turnin' red?" he wanted to know.

"It's not every day," I said, "that I go to Muhammad Ali's, he locks me in the bathroom, then tickles me into submission."

Everyone laughed again. "Ali, you crazy," Rahaman said.

Suddenly, I recognized the obvious: that all afternoon I'd been acting like a teenage admirer again. And that Muhammad Ali had not lost perhaps his most significant talent—the ability to transport people past thoughts and words to a world of feeling and play. Being around Ali, or watching him perform on TV, has always made me feel genuinely childlike. I looked at his family: they were beaming. Ali still flipped their switches, too.

After helping me up, he trudged off to the bathroom. Rahaman crept over from his seat on the sofa and held the door; trying to keep Ali in. The brothers pushed and tugged on the door and, when Ali got out, laughed and wrestled around the room. Then Ali threw several feathery punches at Rahaman and a few at me.

We finally slipped the Ali tape into the VCR. Rahaman brought everyone another root beer and we settled back to watch, he to my left, Ali beside me on the right, and Mrs. Clay beside Ali. The family's reactions to the tape were not unlike those you or I would have, looking at old home movies or the photos in high school yearbooks. Everyone sighed and their mouths arced at tender angles. "Oh, look at Bundini," Mrs. Clay said. "Hey, there's Otis," Rahaman offered.

When there was footage of Ali reciting verse, everyone recited with him. "Those were the days," Rahaman said several times, to which Mrs. Clay responded, "Yes, yes, they were," in a slow, lamenting lilt.

After a half hour or so, she left the room. Rahaman continued to watch the tape for a while, pointing out people and events, but then said he was going to bed. He brought a pen and piece of paper. "Give your name and number," he said, smiling. "We'll look you up."

Then it was just Ali and me. On the TV, it was early 1964 and he was framed on the left by Jim Jacobs and on the right by Drew "Bundini" Brown. "They both dead now," he said, an acute awareness of his own mortality in the tone.

For a time, he continued to stare at the old Ali on the screen, but eventually he lost interest in peering at the distant mountains of his youth. "Did my mom go upstairs? Do you know?" he asked, his voice carrying no further than mine would if I had a hand over my mouth.

"Yeah, I think she's probably asleep."

He nodded, stood, and left the room, presumably to check on her. When he came back, he was moving heavily. His shoulder hit the frame of the door to the kitchen. He went in and came out with two fistfuls of cookies, crumbs all over his mouth. He sat beside me on the sofa. Our knees were touching. Usually, when a man gets this close, I instinctively pull away. He offered a couple of cookies, yawned a giant's yawn, closed his eyes, and seemed to go dead asleep.

"Champ, you want me to leave?" I said. "Am I keeping you up?"

He slowly opened his eyes and was back to our side of The Great Mystery. The pores on his face looked huge, his features elongated, distorted, like someone's in an El Greco. He rubbed his face the way I rub mine when I haven't shaved in a week.

"No, stay," he said. His tone was very gentle.

"You'd let me know if I was staying too late?"

He hesitated only slightly before he answered. "I go to bed at eleven," he said.

With the volume turned this low on the TV, you could hear the videotape's steady whir.

"Can I ask a serious question?" I said. He nodded okay.

"You're still a great man, Champ, I see that. But a lot of people think your mind is fried. Does that bother you?"

He didn't hesitate before answering. "No, there are ignorant people everywhere," he said. "Even educated people can be ignorant."

Does it bother you that you're a great man not being allowed to be great?"

"Wh–wh–whatcha you mean, not allowed to be great?" he said, his voice hardly finding its way out of his body.

"I mean . . . let me think about what I mean . . . I mean the things you seem to care most about, the things you enjoy doing best, the things the rest of us think of as being Muhammad Ali, those are precisely the things that have been taken from you. It just doesn't seem fair."

"You don't question God," he said, his voice rattling in his throat.

"Okay, I respect that, but . . . aw, man, I don't have any business talking to you about this."

"No, no, go on," he said.

"It just bothers me," I told him. I was thinking about the obvious ironies, thinking about Ali continuing to invent, and be invented by, his own mythology. About how he used to talk more easily, and more relentlessly, than anybody in the world (has anyone in history so enjoyed the sweet and spiky melodies of his own voice?); about how he still thought with speed and dazzle, but it took serious effort for him to communicate even with people close to him, including his own mother. About how he may have been the world's best athlete—when walking, he used to move with the mesmeric grace of a leopard turning a corner; now, at night, he stumbled around the house. About how it was his left hand, the same hand from which once slid that great singular Ali snake lick of a jab—the most visible phenomenon of his boxing greatness—the very hand with which he won more than 150 sanctioned fights and tens of thousands of sparring sessions, it's his left hand, not his right, that shook almost continuously. And I was thinking how his major source of pride, his "prettiness,'" remained more or less intact. If Ali lost forty pounds, in the right kind of light, he'd still look classically Greek. The seeming precision with which things have been excised from Ali's life, as well as the gifts that have been left him, sort of spooked me.

"I know why this has happened," Ali said. "God is showing me, and showing you" —he pointed his shaking index finger at me and widened his eyes— "that I'm just a man, just like everybody else."

We sat a long quiet time then, and watched his flickering image on the television screen. It's now 1971 and there was footage of him training for the first Frazier fight. Our Most Public Figure was then The World's Most Beautiful Man and The Greatest Athlete of All Time, his copper skin glowing under the fluorescents, secret rhythms springing in loose firmness from his fingertips.

"Champ, I think it's time for me to go," I said again and made an effort to stand.

"No, stay. You my man," he says, patting my leg. He has always been this way, always wanted to be around people. I take his accolade as one of the greatest compliments of my life.

"I'll tell you a secret," he says, leaning close. "I'm gowna make a comeback."

"What?" I say. I think he's joking, hope he is, but something in his tone makes me uncertain. "You're not serious?" I ask.

And suddenly there is power in his voice. "I'm gowna make a comeback," he repeats louder, more firmly.

"Are you serious?"

"The timing is perfect. They'd think it was a miracle, wouldn't they?" He's speaking distinctly, crisply; he's easy to understand. It's almost the voice I remember from when I first met him in 1975, the one that seemed to come roiling up from down in his belly. In short, Ali sounds like Ali.

"Wouldn't they?" he asks again.

"It would be a miracle," I say.

"Nobody'll take me serious at first. But then I'll get my weight down to two-fifteen and have an exhibition at Yankee Stadium or someplace. Then they'll believe. I'll fight for the title. It'll be bigger than the Resurrection." He stands and walks to the center of the room.

"It'd be good to get your weight down," I say.

"Watch this," he says and dances to his left, studying himself in the mirror above the TV. His new, clean, bright white shoes bound around the carpet; I marvel at how easily he moves. His white clothing accentuates his movements in the dark room; the white appears to make him glow. He starts throwing punches—not the kind he'd tossed at me earlier, but now really letting them go. I'd thought what he'd thrown in the yard was indicative of what he had left. But what he'd done was allow me to play; he'd wanted me to enjoy myself.

"Look at the TV. That's 1971 and I'm just as fast now." One second, two seconds, twelve punches flash in the night. This can't be real. Yet it is. The old man can still do it: he can still make fire appear in the air. He looks faster standing in front of me than do the ghostlike Ali images on the screen. God, I wish I had a video camera to tape this. Nobody would believe me.

"And I'll be even faster when I get my weight down," he tells me.

"You know more now, too," I find myself admitting. Jesus, what am I saying? And why am I saying this? This is a sick man.

"Do you believe?" he asks.

"Well. . . ," I say. *God, the Parkinson's is affecting his sanity. Look at the gray shining in his hair. The guy can hardly walk, for Christ's sake.* Just because he was my boyhood idol doesn't mean I'm blinded to what his life is now like.

And Ali throws another three dozen blows at the gods of mortality, the variety of punches as unpredictable and mesmerizing as starling murmurations. He springs a *triple* hook off of a jab, each punch so quick it trails lines of light, drops straight right leads faster than (most fighters') jabs, erupts into a storm of uppercuts, and the air pops, and his fists and feet whir. This is his best work. His highest art. The very combinations no one has ever thrown quite like Muhammad Ali. When he was fighting, he typically held back some; this is the stuff he seldom *had* to use.

"Do you believe?" he asks, breathing hard.

"They wouldn't let you, even if you could do it," I say, thinking, *There's so much concern everywhere for your health. Everybody thinks they see old Mr. Thanatos waiting for you.*

"Do you *believe*?" he asks again.

"I believe," I hear myself say.

He stops dancing and points a magician's finger at me. Then I get the look, the smile that has closed one hundred thousand interviews.

"April Fool's," he says, sitting down hard beside me again. His mouth is hanging open and his breathing sounds raw. The smell of sweat comes from his skin.

We sit in silence for several minutes. I look at my watch. Its eleven-eighteen. I hadn't realized it was that late. I'd told Lyn I'd be in by eight.

"Champ, I better go home. I have a wife and kids waiting."

"Okay," he says almost inaudibly, looking into the distance, not thinking about me anymore, yawning the kind of long uncovered yawn people usually do among family.

He's bone-tired. I'm tired, too, but I want to leave by saying something that will mean something to him, something that will set me apart from the two billion other people he's met, that will imprint me indelibly in his memory and make the kind of impact on his life that he has made on mine. I want to say the words that will cure his Parkinson's.

Instead I say, "See you Easter, Champ."

He coughs and gives me his hand. "Be cool and look out for the ladies." His words are so volumeless and full of fluid that I don't realize what he's said until I'm halfway out the door.

I don't recall picking up the book he signed, but I must have: its beside my typewriter now. I can't remember walking across his mom's yard and don't remember starting the car. But I do recall what was playing on the tape deck. It was "The Promise of Living" from the orchestral suite to Aaron Copland's *The Tender Land.*

I don't forget Lyn's gallon of milk. Doors to the grocery store whoosh closed behind me. For this time of night, there are quite a few customers in the store. They seem to move more as floating shadows than as people.

An old feeling comes across me that I almost immediately recognize. The sensation is much like going out into the day-to-day world after making love for the first ever time. It's that same sense of having landed in a lesser reality. And of having a secret that the rest of the world can't see.

I reach to grab a milk jug and catch my reflection in the chrome of the dairy counter. There's a half smile on my face and I hadn't realized it.

~

[SEVENTEEN]

The Olympic Torch

By Michael Ezra

The image of Muhammad Ali with the Olympic Torch at the 1996 Atlanta Games is one of the most memorable in all of sport. In this excerpt from his book, Michael Ezra tells the story behind the story.
—K.M.

It had been a long journey for the torch that was going to be used to ignite the cauldron signifying the start of the 1996 Summer Olympics in Atlanta. Some 10,000 people had handled and transported it 15,000 miles over the eighty-four days preceding the games. One of the most successful athletes in Olympic history, Al Oerter, who had won four consecutive gold medals in the discus throw between 1954 and 1968, carried it from just outside what is now known as Turner Field, and through the stadium's bowels before passing it on to a local favorite, boxer Evander Holyfield. Holyfield ran with the torch around the arena's track and then handed it to

Janet Evans, the American gold-medal swimmer, who brought it up a steep ramp toward the cauldron, which loomed high above at the top of a winding trellis.

It appeared that Evans would have the honor of making the final run that would signal the conclusion of the opening ceremonies and the start of the games, but waiting at the top of the ramp was a special guest, ready to deliver the money shot, the moment that the National Broadcasting Company (NBC) hoped would galvanize its $456 million investment in the television rights to the event. In a surprise to all but those connected with the broadcast, amid a huge ovation, Muhammad Ali took the flame from Evans and triggered a mechanism that ignited the cauldron. Trembling and expressionless, but nonetheless a compelling figure, the champion had returned to the world stage as a pop icon. Announcer Bob Costas captured the moment: "Once the most dynamic figure in sports, a gregarious man, now trapped inside that mask created by Parkinson's syndrome. So, in one sense a poignant figure, but look at him, still a great, great presence. Still exuding nobility and stature, and the response he evokes is part affection, part excitement, but especially respect. What a moment." The Ali revolution would be televised after all.

Getting Ali back on television and into the forefront of American cultural consciousness, as Costas's commentary illustrates, was something of a challenge. For an audience that was used to seeing Ali incarnated as a handsome, brash, young, loudmouthed, quick-witted, fleet-footed boxer, the reality of what he had become was sobering. Television is designed to be an entertaining escape from reality. Yet anyone watching Ali struggle to maneuver his torch was reminded that he was having severe physical difficulties, and it would be only natural for audiences to feel bad for him. The question facing the Ali camp, and corporate entities like NBC that wanted to use him for profit, was how to create narratives that would make his rediscovery palatable to viewing audiences. The Ali literary renaissance had provided the script necessary to recast him as a hero to an entire new generation, but if he were to truly catch fire, he would somehow have to be packaged for television in ways that transformed public understanding of his physical condition from a disability to yet another thing that made him great. Ali's lighting of the cauldron was the moment this process began.

Ali's handlers would also need to banish once and for all the lingering images of Ali as a member of the NOI and a black nationalist that distrusted white people. If he was to be recast as an all-American hero rather than an oppositional figure, whatever literary legacy was left by The Greatest would have to be put to rest. Particularly, the story about Ali throwing his gold medal into the Ohio River positioned him outside the mainstream. The story was born at a time when the Ali camp consisted primarily of Herbert Muhammad and the NOI and was exemplary of a black power moment when sticking it to whitey was in vogue. But by 1996 the tale had become a relic that no longer carried the symbolic weight it once had, in addition to being an outright phony. The time had come to set the record straight.

At halftime of the championship basketball game between the United States Dream Team and Yugoslavia, International Olympic Committee Chairman Juan Antonio Samaranch presented Ali with a gold medal to replace the one he had lost. As the crowd roared upon seeing the former champion court-side, Bob Costas clarified for fans what had really happened:

> *There is an apocryphal story that says that Ali, after returning from Rome as a teenager, having brought his country and himself glory, was turned away from restaurants because of segregation, faced racial slurs. That's not apocryphal, that undoubtedly happened. The story goes that in disgust, he took off his medal and threw it into the Ohio River. That is not true. The medal was simply lost. It makes a good symbolic story. It could have happened. It actually did not. But somehow the medal was misplaced. And now that situation will be rectified. Muhammad Ali, who electrified the crowd at the opening ceremony at the Olympic stadium, lighting the Olympic flame, taking the torch from Janet Evans . . . . Although the Parkinson's syndrome*

slows his movements, leaves him virtually unable to speak, he is fully aware of everything that is going on, understands all conversations, understands this reaction, and look at the face, still handsome and smooth, at age fifty-four.

Now the world knew that Ali had not used that most patriotic of symbols, the gold medal, as a protest vehicle. He was back and ready to be marketed. The Olympic appearances successfully reintroduced Ali to television audiences and built upon the momentum that had started with Hauser's literary contributions.

They also controlled proactively the damage that would have stemmed from the botched attempt to bring Ali back to television. A few months earlier, a piece had been taped for an August 4 showing on *60 Minutes*, then the nations highest-ranked television show, which coincided with the Olympic closing ceremonies. Although meant to be a heroic portrayal of the former champion, Ed Bradley's report on Ali was a marketing disaster. It was a classic example of how not to reintroduce Ali to the public, but it also proved to be a valuable lesson to the Ali camp. Its mistakes were never repeated by those who would try to remake Ali into a corporate entity.

The problem with the *60 Minutes* segment was that it highlighted Ali's illness from Parkinson's syndrome without compensating for the pity it was sure to evoke from viewers used to seeing Ali in his prime. While the overall theme was that Ali was dealing with his physical problems gallantly, the piece did not come across as such, despite Bradley's opening monologue:

He called himself "The Greatest" and few argued. For a while he was, quite simply, the most recognizable person in the world. Born Cassius Clay in Louisville, Kentucky, he won his country a gold medal in boxing at the 1960 Olympics and then threw it into the Ohio River as a protest against his country's racism. At fifty-four, it is not surprising that he no longer, as he used to say, floats like a butterfly and stings like a bee. What is surprising about this most famous of all heavyweight champions

> *who ever lived is how he has come to terms with the Parkinson's syndrome that doctors say comes from his years in the ring and by all rights should have laid him low and probably would have if he weren't Muhammad Ali.*

This wasn't a bad start, but the constant emphasis on Ali's physical deterioration compromised the lesson that he was dealing with it heroically. Instead of shifting to Ali's past, as most current visual representations do, the focus remained on the hardships he was facing. While video of Ali at a memorabilia convention rolled, Bradley's voice-over explained: "Today it is increasingly difficult for him to talk. There is a constant shaking of his hands, rigid walk, sometimes a vacant stare. Still, people tend to dismiss his physical limitations and are respectful of the sometimes awkward silence that questions receive."

The middle part of Bradley's report anticipates what would eventually become the commonplace narrative that casts Ali as a mystical and godlike figure. But the *60 Minutes* version does so clumsily, making him appear to be a dying man whose soul has left his body and is operating on a different plane than that of mere mortals. There are several references to Ali's seeing his good deeds—signing complimentary autographs, praying, making charity pilgrimages to impoverished areas of the world -- as a means for him to get into heaven. It would be only natural for a viewer to be more concerned for his well-being than convinced of his transcendence. On the other hand, there are also some great illustrations of how Ali is still able to conjure up his own special brand of charisma under debilitating circumstances: doing magic tricks that impressed Fidel Castro, maintaining business interests that at the time earned him almost $1 million annually, and, in a beautiful and hilarious moment, convincing Bradley that he suffered from a sleep disorder that caused him to throw punches while unconscious.

Bradley's unsuccessful attempt to interview Ali at the end of the segment could have been disastrous to the former fighter's future currency as a corporate pitchman. Seated under the television lights,

Ali backed out at the last minute after hearing Bradley's first question. "Can't do it," he said and walked off camera. Clearly shaken, Bradley explained to viewers that Ali didn't want his speech impediment to make people feel sorry for him, but that was exactly what the scene accomplished. Despite all the heroic rhetoric about Ali's ability to cope with his illness like the champion of old, the moment proved that he was having trouble coming to terms with his physical state.

In their attempt to undo the prevailing sadness, the final scenes wind up exacerbating the pathos. Asked about the situation, Lonnie Ali says, "I think he is very aware of how he sounds, and coming from where Muhammad from, the Louisville Lip, and being as audible and as boastful as he used to be when he was boxing. I mean, he was always talking. And now to have a problem with his voice and speaking, I think it bothers him a great deal." To the follow-up question asking whether the former champ was embarrassed by his condition, Lonnie replied, "I would say yes, to some degree he is."

Although the final images of the piece show Ali hitting a heavy bag in a manner that suggests he could knock out any regular person standing in the way of his punch, they are drowned out by Lonnie Ali's last words. Although meant to convince viewers of her husband's well-being, Lonnie's statement sounded more like something that someone would utter about a terminally ill relative eking out his final years in an assisted-living facility: "Muhammad is very well taken care of. He is a very independent individual, probably always will be until the day he dies. He makes his own decisions. He's not destitute. There are people who are more deserving of the public's sympathy than Muhammad. Muhammad is a happy man."

The *60 Minutes* piece did not abort the Ali television revolution; actually, it wound up helping it. When an advance copy of the segment landed in the hands of Dick Ebersol, the president of NBC Sports, it inspired him to push for Ali to become the centerpiece of his network's coverage of the Summer Olympics. Ali's surprise emergence at the opening ceremonies was a made-for-television event, as evidenced by the intrigue surrounding negotiations to bring him on board. About a fortnight beforehand, he flew to Atlanta for a secret, pre-dawn rehearsal. Then, to fool those who might be suspicious of his presence in the city around the time of the Olympics, Ali returned about a week later to attend a United States Olympic Committee dinner. This visit gave him an excuse for being in town if anyone asked what he was doing there. Howard Bingham accompanied Ali, serving as the Ali's camp's representative. His job was to make sure that NBC would not aggravate the damage that was potentially looming as a result of the *60 Minutes* telecast. After Ali agreed to take part in the production, both he and Bingham signed confidentiality agreements to ensure that the event would have maximum impact.

The deal culminated Ebersol's six months of lobbying real estate lawyer Billy Payne, who as chairman of the Atlanta Committee for the Olympic Games had final say on who would light the cauldron. Payne favored Evander Holyfield, the Atlanta native, evangelical Christian, and former world heavyweight champion, for the honor. "Billy didn't have a real fundamental appreciation of Ali beyond his being a boxer, and about his life now. Billy wanted to know what he represented now," said Ebersol. In an effort to change his mind Ebersol sent Payne a campaign package that included the *60 Minutes* piece. But the segment raised doubts about whether Ali was an appropriate choice and whether he was physically up to the role. Payne, along with Don Mishner, the executive director of the opening ceremonies, met with Howard Bingham to discuss Ali's condition. "They wanted to know if Ali physically could do it," said Bingham. "I told them Ali can do anything he wants to do." Ebersol added, "Muhammad knew how it was going to be lit, that he wouldn't have to run up any stairs," as was customary for many people in that position to do. Ali, too, had doubts. "Initially, Muhammad had reservations about doing it because he doesn't like the image he projects on television and he realized that billions of people around the world would see him. But then he also realized this was a way to help deliver his message of tolerance and understanding," said Thomas Hauser. Believing that it was his moral duty to accept the honor, Ali anticipated the symbolic benefits of his participation:

"Mankind coming together. Martin Luther King's home. Muslims seeing me with the torch."

It was a critical moment for the legacy of Muhammad Ali, marking his evolution from public figure to icon. The responses to Ali's selection and the event's execution were overwhelmingly positive, triggering a new and uplifting surge of affection toward him. George Vecsey of the *New York Times* wrote, "Muhammad Ali floats above the Summer Games, no longer an elusive butterfly but a great glowing icon as large as a spaceship. He casts his light on every athlete, every spectator, every volunteer, all the people who walk these humid streets with just a little more zip in their step, now that they have seen Ali." For those who had been wondering what had become of Ali, or were troubled by rumors that he was dying, this moment was comforting. Certainly, Vecsey noticed, there was trepidation among the viewing audience: "Nobody wanted Ali to be remembered as the weakened legend who dropped the Olympic torch in front of billions of people around the world . . . . Hang on to the torch, Ali. That's what we said in my section." Ali's overcoming his physical problems to complete the task at hand translated into a sign of his transcendent moral authority, his ability to bring the races together, and his symbolizing the infinite possibilities of life:

> *Putting him on that platform was a stroke of genius that transformed a very nice ceremony into a celebration, a block party. I was sitting with a black male colleague and a white female colleague, and when we saw Ali shining on that platform, we exchanged high-fives at the audacious perfection of it. Ali was at the Games. Ali was on the hill. Raise the flame. Float like a butterfly, sting like a bee, all of us.*

Even President Bill Clinton, on hand to declare an official start to the games, was deeply moved when he saw the former champ. Embracing him, he said, "They didn't tell me who would light the flame, but when I saw it was you, I cried." Yes, Ali still invoked pity in some people, but overall, his ability to do himself proud despite obstacles was seen as inspirational. That he had achieved yet another unlikely victory, as he had against Liston and Foreman, brought a sense of hope to people. This sentiment would eventually be harnessed at the center of a 2004 advertising campaign by the sneaker company Adidas. The ad featured Ali and the tagline, "Impossible is nothing."

Over a decade later, the impact of Ali's Olympic moment endures. The sports television network ESPN recently declared it the eighth most memorable moment in the past twenty-five years of sports. The event solidified Ali's standing as a moral force and American hero, a representative of his country on the world stage. During the next ten years, Ali received an avalanche of honors recognizing his national and international significance. In 1998, he was given the United Nations Messenger of Peace award. In Atlanta three years later, he became the initial torchbearer in the months-long processional that would culminate in the lighting of the cauldron to open the 2002 Olympic Games in Salt Lake City. In 2005, he traveled to Singapore to represent New York's campaign to host the 2012 Summer Games. Michael Bloomberg, the city's mayor, referenced Ali's Olympic past in a press statement:

> *We are deeply honored that Muhammad Ali [is] part of the New York delegation in Singapore for the IOC [International Olympic Committee] Host City election. In 1996, Muhammad Ali's courageous lighting of the Olympic caldron was one of the most powerful displays of the Olympic spirit ever. We are forever in awe of this great man who transcends all divides and touches us all. His athletic ability, indomitable spirit and grace have been an inspiration to tens of millions around the world.*

The cauldron lighting proved that Muhammad Ali, if used correctly, was a powerful force that could drive the most important of made-for-television events. NBC had taken a huge financial gamble by using him, and its investment paid off royally. Over the next decade, Ali's career as an endorser, built around the themes of morality, inspiration, achievement, and perseverance, would reach unprecedented heights. In the meantime, his literary legacy was also evolving, as the notion of Ali as moral authority was developing into something far greater, the idea of Ali as godlike.

~

Excerpt from "Olympic Torch: From Literature to Television" from Muhammad Ali: The Making of an Icon by Michael Ezra. Used by permission of Temple University Press.

[EIGHTEEN]

The Greatest Tribute

By Bill Plaschke

Ali had been carefully involved in the planning of his own funeral. Working with his wife, closest friends and Islamic scholars, they laid out all the details in a document so thick they began calling it "The Book." He was laid to rest on June 10, 2016. —K.M.

The day began where Muhammad Ali's life began, on the Louisville city streets, a simple black hearse adorned with "A.D. Porter and Sons" giving the champ one last parade for his people.

From his boyhood home at Grand Avenue to his final resting place at the Cave Hill Cemetery, through littered lots and gleaming buildings filled with unconditional love, Ali's funeral procession Friday morning spanned 74 years, 19 miles and countless tears that streaked beneath sweat towels and sunglasses

"A-li, A-li, A-li," chanted the hundreds of sweltering folks as they crowded the corner of Muhammad Ali Boulevard and Ninth Street, reaching arms toward the unadorned black car as if believing The Greatest was still alive and smiling and dancing inside.

Hours later, the day ended as Muhammad Ali's life was lived, with a raucous and passionate memorial service in a glittering basketball arena on a muddy Ohio River whose bridges he once walked with his dreams.

"I am Muhammad Ali," chanted the crowd in the overflow arena at the KFC Yum! Center, answering the urgings of Rabbi Joe Rapport, one of the many speakers of many faiths who turned the service into a pep rally for humanity.

Ali, the former three-time heavyweight champion and world's most impactful athlete who died last week at age 74 after a three-decade battle with Parkinson's disease, rested amid a wonderful absence of quiet on a day he would have loved.

He floated through the city as if on the wings of a butterfly, then he was the focus of a series of uplifting and challenging tributes that stung like a bee.

"You shook up the world in life, and now you're shaking up the world in death," said Rasheda Ali-Walsh, one of Ali's nine children. "Daddy is looking down at us, right? Saying, 'I told you I was the greatest!'"

The procession was indeed the greatest, a morning-long preamble through a crowd of about 100,000 folks who hugged and wept and threw flowers on the hearse after leaving the local funeral home.

"He gave so much to the world, he taught us we could do anything," said Clinton Bacon, a construction worker standing and sweating on the corner of Ali and Ninth.

The ensuing memorial service, which fittingly started an hour late, much like most Ali championship fights, was also the greatest. There were prayers from representatives of a half-dozen faiths and denominations. There were nine eulogies, including Ali's widow Lonnie, former President Bill Clinton and comedian Billy Crystal. But more than anything, there was a connection, with fans responding to the words with not only standing ovations, but isolated shouts, extended personal monologues, and at least one solitary song.

President Clinton called Ali, "a universal soldier for our common humanity," and it was this sort of humanity that Ali embraced on a day that he had been planning for 10 years.

Clinton wasn't the only president whose voice was heard.

"Muhammad Ali was America—brash, defiant, pioneering, joyful, never tired, always game to test the odds," wrote President Barack Obama in a letter read by senior White House adviser Valerie Jarrett.

Just as the dignitaries were folks from a variety of backgrounds, so were the fans. The Yum! Center lobby filled with a mix of women in prayer garb, families wearing matching T-shirts adorned with Ali photos, and old guys chomping on burned cigars arguing about Sonny Liston.

Tickets for the service were free, snapped up two days earlier by fans who showed up in the middle of the night and still couldn't believe their luck.

Angela Lucear, a local administrative assistant, showed up at 4:30 a.m., reached the box office several hours later, and still remembers the strange words.

"They said, 'You want four tickets? Here's four. Take them. Have a nice day,'" Lucear recalled. "I was like, Yay!"

Lucear, was surprised again when she walked inside and looked for concession stands. Ali had determined that nothing would be sold, so tables around the arena were filled with bottled water and snacks like Flamin' Hot Cheetos to Scooby-Doo! Graham cracker sticks.

"I was like, wait a minute, this is all free?" Lucear said. "But that was Ali, right? There will never be anybody like him."

The inclusion preached by Ali was obvious when looking at the inside of the arena, where the regular seats were filled while luxury suites were empty. The fight waged by Ali then became clear with the first speaker, Dr. Kevin Cosby, a local preacher, who praised Ali for being a black American icon.

"He dared to love black people at a time when black people had trouble loving themselves," Cosby said before loudly chided those who once gave up on the champ.

"A lot of people bet on Muhammad Ali when he was in the winner's circle," Cosby said, comparing Ali's life to the Kentucky Derby. "But the masses bet on him when he was still in the mud."

The service was filled with similar pronouncements about the message of Ali's life, which he began here as Cassius Clay before winning the heavyweight championship, embraced the Muslim faith and changed his name to Muhammad Ali.

He was stripped of his title in 1967 for refusing to fight in the Vietnam War, then, after spending nearly four years in boxing exile while refusing to disavow his beliefs, he returned to the ring and became champion two more times before fighting for the final time in 1981.

"He decided he would never be disempowered," said President Clinton. "He decided not his race nor his place would strip from him the power to write his own story."

Ali made an even bigger impact after his retirement as he traveled the world preaching peace and philanthropy. Much of Friday's service, in fact focused on those years. There were no boxing videos. There were no boxing photos. There were no speeches from anyone involved in Ali's boxing life.

This was clearly intended as a memorial for a statesman, not a sportsman.

"The first part of his life was dominated by the triumph of his truly unique gifts . . . the second part of his life was more important," Clinton said. "In the second half of his life he perfected gifts that we all have . . . gifts of mind and heart."

When the day ended, and the Ali chants quieted, the crowd filed out into warmth of downtown streets where even the city buses had only one destination.

"Ali—The Greatest," scrolled the marquee over one.

The Greatest indeed saved the greatest for last.

"I think Muhammad had something to do with all this," said Lonnie Ali. "Even in death, Muhammad has something to say."

[PART TWO]

Reflections on Muhammad Ali

[NINETEEN]

"Ali Will Always Be America"

By President Barack Obama

President Obama was unable to attend Ali's funeral because it conflicted with his daughter Malia's high school graduation. Senior advisor Valerie Jarrett attended the funeral and read the following tribute from the president and first lady. —K.M.

~

It was 1980, and an epic career was in its twilight. Everybody knew it, probably including The Champ himself. Ali went into one of his final fights an underdog; all the smart money was on the new champ, Larry Holmes. And in the end, the oddsmakers were right.

A few hours later, at 4 a.m., after the loss, after all the fans had gone, a sportswriter asked a restroom attendant if he'd bet on the fight. The man—black, getting on in years—said he'd put his money on Ali. The writer asked why.

"Why?" he said. "Why? Because he's Muhammad Ali, that's why. Mister, I'm 72 years old. I owe the man for giving me my dignity."

To Lonnie and the Ali family, President Clinton, and an arena full of distinguished guests—the man we celebrate today was not just a boxer, or a poet, or an agitator, or a man of peace. He was not just a Muslim, or a black man, or a Louisville kid. He wasn't even just "The Greatest of All Time."

He was Muhammad Ali, a whole greater than the sum of its parts. He was bigger, brighter, more original and influential than just about anyone of his era. You couldn't have made him up. And yes, he was pretty, too.

He had fans in every city and village and ghetto on the planet; he was feted by foreign heads of state; the Beatles' British invasion took a detour to come to him. It seemed sometimes that The Champ was simply too big for America.

But I actually think the world flocked to him in wonder precisely because, as he once put it, Muhammad Ali was America. Brash, defiant, pioneering, joyful, never tired, always game to test the odds. He was our most basic freedoms—religion, speech, spirit. He embodied our ability to invent ourselves. His life spoke to our original sin of slavery and discrimination, and the journey he traveled helped to shock our conscience and lead us on a roundabout path toward salvation. And, like America, he was always very much a work in progress.

We'd do him a disservice to gauze up his story, to sand down his rough edges, to talk only of floating butterflies and stinging bees. Ali was a radical even in a radical's time; a loud, proud, unabashedly black voice in a Jim Crow world.

His jabs knocked some sense into us, pushing us to expand our imaginations and bring others into our understanding. There were times he swung a bit wildly, wounding the wrong opponent, as he was the first to admit. But through all his triumphs and failures, Ali seemed to achieve the sort of enlightenment, an inner peace, that we're all striving toward.

In the '60s, when other young men his age were leaving the country to avoid the war or jail, he was asked why he didn't join them. He got angry. He said he'd never leave—his people are here, the millions "struggling for freedom, and justice, and equality . . . . I can do a lot to help, in jail or not."

He'd have everything stripped from him—his titles, his standing, his money, his passion, very nearly his freedom. But Ali still chose America. I imagine he knew that only here, in this country, could he win it all back. So he chose to help perfect a union where a descendant of slaves can become the king of the world, and in the process, lend some dignity to all of us—maids, porters, students, maybe even an elderly bathroom attendant—and help inspire a young mixed kid with a funny name to have the audacity to believe he could be anything, even President of the United States.

Muhammad Ali was America. He will always be America.

What a man. What a spirit. What a joyous, mighty champion.

God bless The Greatest of All Time. God bless his family. And God bless the nation we love.

[TWENTY]

The Real Ali the Mythologizers Ignore

By Jack Cashill

Most people—even our heroes—are neither all good or nor all bad. But when our heroes die, we tend to focus on the good. In the following article from conservative news site WND, Jack Cashill takes the opposite approach. He is author of Sucker Punch: The Left Hook that Dazed Ali and Killed King's Dream. —K.M.

~

"Do you believe that lynching is the answer to interracial sex?" the Playboy interviewer asked Muhammad Ali. "A black man should be killed if he's messing with a white woman," answered Ali.

"And what if a Muslim woman wants to go out with non-Muslim blacks—or white men, for that matter?" asked the interviewer. Said Ali, "Then she dies. Kill her, too."

This interview took place in 1975, when Ali was 33 years old, and youth was no excuse. The media chose not to hear. They had long since lionized Ali and were hellbent on sanctifying him.

Despite his seeming racism, Muhammad Ali had a fundamentally decent core. Beyond that, he was clever, charismatic, charming, entertaining, a gifted boxer and, in the ring at least, as courageous as any sane man could be.

From the years 1964 to at least 1975, however, he was a mess, and the media steadfastly refused to notice. In the way of example, star sportswriter Roger Kahn praised Ali for "his crystal sense of the irrationality and the cruelty of the society" in the very same year Ali sanctioned the lynching of interracial couples.

The media could never acknowledge what wife Sonji did, namely that Ali was not "his own master." For those paying attention, the Playboy interview confirmed as much.

Ali belonged heart and soul to the Nation of Islam, an outfit Malcolm X had sadly concluded was a nation of "zombies" — "hypnotized, pointed in a certain direction and told to march."

Giving the marching orders was NOI honcho Elijah Muhammad. During World War II, Muhammad dodged the draft and actively collaborated with the Axis powers.

When faced with the draft in 1967, Ali yielded to the pressure the anti-white, anti-American Muhammad brought to bear. There was little courage involved, less principle, and no sign at all of independent thought.

Right before the Zora Folley fight, his last before his exile from boxing, Ali called boxing great Sugar Ray Robinson and asked if he could come see him at his New York hotel. Robinson obliged. Ali wanted to talk about the Army.

"You've got to go," said Robinson.

"No," Ali answered, "Elijah Muhammad told me that I can't go."

Robinson explained the consequences of his refusal, and Ali answered, "But I'm afraid, Ray. I'm real afraid."

When Robinson asked if he was afraid of the Muslims, Ali refused to answer. "His eyes were glistening with tears," Robinson reported, "tears of torment, tears of indecision."

Ali had good reason to be afraid. Muhammad was not a man to be trifled with. Soon after Ali joined the NOI, he had Ali's former mentor, Malcolm X, assassinated. Ali had been too scared to intervene.

Happy to make Ali a pariah, Muhammad unwittingly made Ali the patron saint of the ascendant left. Ali's authoritative biographer, Thomas Hauser, admitted as much.

The anti-war movement, said Hauser, saved the young Ali from the "ugly" mood of the Nation of Islam just as Ali was adopting "the Nation's persona and its ideology."

Hauser argued that "when the spotlight turned from Ali's acceptance of an ideology that sanctioned hate to his refusal to accept induction into the U.S. Army, Ali began to bond with the white liberal community, which at the time was quite strong."

Although Ali's manic racial ideology unnerved old-school liberals, the young anti-war crowd proved much more morally flexible, and as Hauser admitted, this faction was "quite strong."

That faction was strong enough and blind enough to ignore the "ugly" side of Ali's life. Had Ali not become a reluctant anti-war symbol, he never would have become a symbol of racial healing.

After Muhammad died and the NOI collapsed, Ali turned his life around. If proof were needed, he attended the Republican National Convention as a Reagan supporter in 1984, a fact that drives his mythologizers nuts.

Ali's glory years, however, were a moral disaster. A summing up of this period of his life sheds some useful light both on the young Ali and the media that made him:

- Ali knowingly betrayed Malcolm X, a betrayal that led at least indirectly to Malcolm's assassination.
- Ali publicly turned his back on his press secretary, Leon 4X Ameer, which led even more directly to Ameer's death.
- When Nation of Islam activists executed five friends and family of the Hanafi sect—four of them children—in the D.C. home of Kareem Abdul-Jabbar, Ali did not quit the Nation or even publicly protest.
- For at least four years running, Ali publicly degraded Joe

Frazier, often along the crudest racial lines. "There's a great honor about Joe," said baseball great Reggie Jackson. "That was evident in the way he fought. And Muhammad ridiculed Joe; he humiliated him in front of the world."

- Ali was an unapologetic sexist. "In the Islamic world," he told Playboy in 1975, "the man's the boss, and the woman stays in the background. She don't want to call the shots." Feminists still wrestle over this one.
- Ali left four of his children without a father in the home after rejecting their Muslim mother for a more glamorous, lighter skinned 18-year-old.
- Ali routinely denigrated black heroes who did not share his point of view—Joe Louis, Jackie Robinson and Thurgood Marshall among them.
- Ali shamelessly courted some of the most brutal dictators on the planet: Gadhafi, Amin, Duvalier, Nkrumah, Mobutu, Marcos.

Why have so many people right of center yielded to the Ali myth? Boxer Larry Holmes knew the answer. "He wasn't a saint," said Holmes. "But if you tell people something like that they kick your a—. You can't talk bad about Muhammad Ali."

~

"The real Ali the mythologizers ignore," Jack Cashill, June 8, 2016. Licensed from WND.

[TWENTY-ONE]

What Made Ali 'The Greatest' in the Ring?

By Alan Hahn

Alan Hahn is adjunct professor at the University of Canberra.

Many factors came together to create recognition of Muhammad Ali, who has died aged 74, as "the greatest" boxer in history.

There is no doubt Ali's determination to overcome racial inequality, his refusal to fight in the Vietnam War, his emergence as a representative of Islam and his highly engaging media persona coalesced to make him by far the most widely known boxer of all time. He came to be popularly regarded as a champion of the oppressed and a seeker of justice for the persecuted. This resonated globally.

Central to the celebrity Ali achieved, though, was his exceptional ability as a boxer.

A unique style

Various boxing authorities have ranked Ali as the best heavyweight boxer in history. He and the legendary Sugar Ray Robinson have been bracketed as the top two across all weight divisions.

Ali won a gold medal (as a light heavyweight) at the 1960 Rome Olympics as the culmination of an amateur boxing career in which he won 100 of 105 bouts.

As a professional, Ali won the world heavyweight championship on three separate occasions over 14 years. He was victorious in 56 of 61 professional bouts, with three of the losses coming late in his career when his athleticism had faded. *Sports Illustrated* named him as its Sportsman of the 20th Century.

What made Ali such an outstanding exponent of his sport?

It certainly wasn't sheer strength and power. He was never considered to be among boxing's hardest punchers and more than one-third of his professional contests lasted their full scheduled duration. Nor was he remarkable in terms of height or weight.

Rather, Ali's speed, agility, footwork and general athleticism were among the attributes that most distinguished him from other competitors. It was said he was a heavyweight who moved like a lightweight

In the early years of his career, Ali also displayed outstanding aerobic endurance: he was able to relentlessly maintain his dancing, up-on-the-toes style.

There is no doubt Ali was uniquely skilled. But he employed techniques that, while clearly effective, were far from classical. In stark contrast to contemporary views of best practice, he often held his hands by his sides at waist level, and he sometimes avoided the punches of opponents by pulling his head backwards away from them

Many boxing experts regarded these as high-risk behaviours made viable only by Ali's astonishing speed, but the unorthodoxy served to confuse his adversaries and lure them into errors. He was seldom the aggressor, preferring a method that capitalised on the aggression of others.

Ali very aptly characterised his own style as "float like a butterfly, sting like a bee". His distinctive, unconventional boxing style was in keeping with the fierce individualism and rejection of norms that pervaded other aspects of his life and created almost universal interest in him.

Mental strength

Ali also demonstrated major psychological strengths. He was renowned for his self-belief, which frequently extended beyond vociferous pre-contest expressions of confidence to actually nominating the very round in which he would win.

He was predisposed to composing rap-style poems designed to extol his talents and unsettle opponents, and was well-known for his intimidatory stares and for subjecting opponents to verbal taunts during bouts.

Over time, Ali's perennial competitive success seemed increasingly to justify the self-belief and enabled him to inculcate an impression that he was almost superhuman. That was an impression that a public seeking new heroes in turbulent social and political times was very willing to accept. In addition, it appears to have been embraced by Ali himself.

The self-belief and illusion of superhuman qualities were arguably instrumental in enabling Ali to get through a number of torturous contests. These included the "Thrilla in Manila", where he and Joe Frazier inflicted shocking damage on each other in what he later described as a near-death experience, and the "Rumble in the Jungle".

In the Rumble in the Jungle, Ali absorbed some massively forceful punches from George Foreman as part of a contrived "rope-a-dope" strategy. This eventually brought him an unlikely victory that proved to be the crowning glory of his incredible boxing journey.

In the phase of his boxing career commencing after his 3½-year suspension from the sport due to his refusal to enter the US Armed Forces, Ali became famous for an extraordinary ability to "take a punch". This—along with the courage and commitment to purpose that it implies—has been viewed as another reason for his boxing greatness.

The taking of punches, though, very likely had a significant downside in causing neurological injury and contributing to the Parkinson's disease that affected his life from the mid-1980s onwards and was soon greatly debilitating.

Ali not only competed during the "golden years of heavyweight boxing" but was the fundamental reason for them. He brought completely new dimensions to the sport and gave it a sort of aestheticism and a broader relevance that was without precedent.

Despite the health problems that he suffered in retirement, he reportedly continued to enjoy being Muhammad Ali. That enjoyment was well-earnt. He inspired and empowered multitudes of people around the world and engendered cultural change.

Ali's passing has evoked widespread sadness, particularly among the many admirers who somehow identified so strongly with him that they felt a quite intensively personal sharing of his triumphs and defeats, both in the ring and outside it. He leaves an enduring and highly influential legacy, that in the final analysis has been made possible by the qualities that made him genuinely "the greatest" as a boxer.

"What Made Muhammad Ali 'The Greatest' in the ring?" Alan Hahn. This article was originally published in The Conversation.

[TWENTY-TWO]

Muhammad Ali and Black Lives Matter

By Janaya Khan

Janaya Khan is the co-founder of Black Lives Matter Toronto.

For years I woke up at 6am, still feeling tightness in my body from the previous night's sparring session. I would throw on a sweater, eat oatmeal, and take a bus, a train, and another bus back to my gym. In my hand, a battered copy of Alex Haley's The Autobiography of Malcolm X.

The week before, I had been reading about Elijah Muhammad. I learned of these people through researching everything I could find on Muhammad Ali. He is the reason I started to box. I first heard his name when he lit the Olympic Torch in 1996, and as I learned of the boxer, I learned more about his politics and struggles.

Muhammad Ali started boxing at the age of 12, and by 18 had won Olympic gold. At 22, he defeated the fearsome Sonny Liston to become the youngest heavyweight champion of the world. He converted to Islam shortly thereafter through the Nation of Islam, and by his second fight with Liston he had renounced his former name. By 1965, his friend Malcolm X had been assassinated. In 1966, he refused to be inducted into the Vietnam War. Ali was no longer just the heavyweight champion of the world, he was black and Muslim and something very threatening to white America.

Consequently he was stripped of his prime boxing years; his belts were forfeited and his boxing licence was denied between 1967 and 1970. In that time, Martin Luther King Jr was assassinated.

Ali became a critical voice in anti-war and black resistance movements alike in his clear articulation of racism, imperialism and his refusal to become respectable to appease white expectations. After fighting three monumental bouts against then champion Joe Frazier, ultimately losing his title belt, he fought the powerful George Foreman in Zaire (now the Democratic Republic of Congo) to reclaim it.

It was at this point that Ali reached legendary status across the world. He had been proclaiming it for decades throughout his record-setting career, but now the world was proclaiming it, too; Muhammad Ali: The Greatest.

Like Ali, I became politicised through pugilism. The first boxing gym I entered was largely made up of lesbian and queer-identified women, trans people and survivors of violence. When I moved on to another boxing gym led by a young racialised woman to focus more on competitive boxing, I had actualised into a queer, gender non-conforming boxer and organiser.

Boxing was the skill I was most eager to share as my sense of activism grew and the need to protect ourselves as queer, trans and female-identified people on the front lines became more and more apparent. I would lug a huge bag of boxing gloves and a set of hand pads to any conference or congregation of activists I could get to. I would teach oppressed people how to throw punches and defend themselves, and sit in on workshops led by powerhouses in the movement to learn.

The Movement for Black Lives is today's iteration and continuation of the Black Power movements that formed in the 1960s.

Black Lives Matter (BLM) was created when 17-year-old Trayvon Martin was murdered by police in 2013 in Florida, and has since developed into both an international movement and a network. I have been active in BLM since its conception, and I and a powerful team started the Black Lives Matter movement in Canada.

As with Ali, boxing led me along a path that allowed me to contribute to the tradition of black resistance. Our generation is fighting many of the same issues that affected Ali and his generation—police brutality, white supremacy, poverty, imperialism and Islamophobia. We are also grappling with many of the same questions around the best strategies for black liberation, from the role of assimilation with the reality of anti-black racism as a hegemonic pillar, to the role of economy and participation in electoral politics.

The lessons I gleaned from boxing, my coach, and fighters such as Ali, inform how I theorise and organise. The number one rule in boxing is "Protect yourself at all times".

This lesson is integral in my relationship to direct actions and a necessary framework for many of us who either identify as women or were socialised as women. A boxer is most open to punches when they are throwing punches themselves, and Ali was the champion of "make them miss, make them pay". This, like protecting ourselves and each other, has become a parable in how I organise, write and box.

I now do international work for Black Lives Matter, and my connections to many different movement contexts have allowed me to witness the extent to which the loss of Muhammad Ali has affected millennials and elders alike globally. Stories have been shared that dig deeper into his legacy, from being exploited by promoters and hanger-ons to resisting the mainstream media's efforts to downplay his black and Muslim identities. Numerous compilation videos of his fights have emerged, interviews and quotations that show his political stance, and books that shed light on his relationship to and evolution beyond the Nation of Islam make it clear that his legacy is just as meaningful now as it was when he held the belt over his head in triumph.

This has been a difficult year in losing black giants. From

Afeni Shakur, mother and freedom fighter, to Prince, a redefiner of black masculinity, musician and active supporter of Black Lives Matter, to Ali. We are finding ourselves called upon to pick up their tools and continue the fight.

My first and truest tools are a pair of boxing gloves, and I have Ali to thank for that. Ali, whose accomplishments were too great for the four corners of the ring to hold. Ali, who brought to light many of the contradictions of white supremacy. Ali, a teacher on the responsibility that comes with greatness.

~

"Muhammad Ali and Black Lives Matter," Janaya Khan, June 12, 2016. Licensed from Al Jazeera.

[TWENTY-THREE]

America's Most Famous Muslim

By Bobby Ilich

Bobby Ilich is sports editor for the International Business Times.

The faith of Muhammad Ali has been among the most contentious elements of the famed boxer's life. Perhaps the most prominent public figure in modern times to convert from Christianity to Islam, Ali caused a stir when he changed his name from Cassius Marcellus Clay Jr. in 1964, but he has had an evolving relationship with the Muslim faith.

"They call it the Black Muslims," said a 22-year-old Clay at the time. "This is a press word. It is not a legitimate name. But Islam is a religion, and there are 750 million people all over the world who believe in it, and I am one of them."

After defeating Sonny Liston by a technical knockout in a controversial heavyweight title fight, Ali would join the Nation of Islam, whose doctrines of racial separation deviate from orthodox Islam.

But he would later convert to mainstream Sunni Islam in 1975, and then to the Sufi sect in 2005.

In the recently released book "Blood Brothers," historians Randy Roberts and Johnny Smith chronicled the intense friendship of Muhammad Ali and social activist Malcolm X, who had "magnetized Clay, drawing him toward the inner circle of the Nation."

In the early 1960s, there was a fear from Ali's camp that his relationship with the Nation of Islam would jeopardize his chances of a shot at the heavyweight title. Not only did Ali fight and defeat Liston, he would later emerge as a political figure in 1967 for refusing induction into the armed forces during the Vietnam War, and leading to a three-year suspension.

"The relationship between Cassius Clay and Malcolm X signaled a new direction in American culture, one shaped by the forces of sports and entertainment, race and politics," Roberts and Smith wrote. "Under Malcolm's tutelage, [Ali] embraced the world stage, emerging as an international symbol of black pride and black independence. Without Malcolm, Muhammad Ali would have never become the 'king of the world.'"

But when Malcolm X broke away from the Nation of Islam, the friendship with Ali also broke off. After Malcolm X was assassinated in 1965, Ali expressed regret that he never had the chance to mend the friendship, according to Roberts and Smith.

In a Facebook posting, Yasir Qadhi, a professor of religious studies at Rhodes College in Memphis, Tennessee, fondly detailed Ali's positive influence on American Muslims.

"If the only good that he brought was to bring a positive image of Islam, and to spread the name of our beloved Prophet (SAW) in every household and on every tongue in the world, it is a life that is indeed enviable," Qadhi wrote. He praised Ali's "positive political activism" and "preaching truth to power."

"He converted to what he thought was Islam at a time when Islam was an unknown religion; then he became Sunni after Malcolm X introduced him to mainstream Islam, and he's been a proud and public Muslim ever since."

As recently as December, Ali maintained his role as proponent for Muslim rights. He addressed Republican presidential candidate Donald Trump's controversial stance on halting immigration of Muslims with a statement that had the headline: "Presidential Candidates Proposing to Ban Muslim Immigration to the United States."

Ali did not mention Trump by name, but it was clear that his intention was to promote a positive image of Muslims and denounce radical Islam and ties to terrorism.

"I am a Muslim and there is nothing Islamic about killing innocent people in Paris, San Bernardino, or anywhere else in the world. True Muslims know that the ruthless violence of so called Islamic Jihadists goes against the very tenets of our religion.

"We as Muslims have to stand up to those who use Islam to advance their own personal agenda. They have alienated many from learning about Islam. True Muslims know or should know that it goes against our religion to try and force Islam on anybody.

"Speaking as someone who has never been accused of political correctness, I believe that our political leaders should use their position to bring understanding about the religion of Islam and clarify that these misguided murderers have perverted people's views on what Islam really is."

~

"America's Most Famous Muslim," Bobby Ilich, June 2, 2016. Licensed from International Business Times.

[TWENTY-FOUR]

Ali Rewrote the Rules for Athletes as Activists

By David Rowe

David Rowe is professor of cultural research at the Institute for Culture and Society at Western Sydney University.

~

The descriptor "icon" is vastly overused in these celebrity-fixated times, but it could have been invented for Muhammad Ali, who has died aged 74. Thirty-five years after he threw his last punch in the ring, Ali is still front of mind in any discussion of the most-important sportsman ever.

He does not occupy this status because he is widely regarded as the best boxer there has ever been, who narcissistically called himself "The Greatest", and then forced a reluctant boxing world to agree. Ali was much bigger than boxing. He came, from the late 1960s onwards, to symbolise resistance to racism, militarism and inequality.

He embodied the intimate relationship between sport and politics that so troubles those, like nationalistic politicians, who deny its existence while ruthlessly exploiting it.

So how did Ali so consistently receive the kind of acclaim heaped on him by human rights activist and sports scholar Richard E. Lapchick, who describes Ali as "not a one-in-a million figure, but a once-in-a-lifetime person"?

Ali was a superlative boxer, but it was his great physical beauty and quick wit that made a major impression on those who knew little of boxing or were repelled by its brutality. Under his birth name, Cassius Clay, he forced himself into public consciousness by theatrically talking up his "prettiness", athletic brilliance and verbal facility.

From early in his career he self-consciously played the role of anti-hero with a racial twist. Knowing the white-dominated boxing establishment and fan base were always searching, especially in the prestigious heavyweight division, for a "great white hope" to put African-American champions in their place, Ali goaded them to find him another fighter to beat.

Decades before sportspeople used social media to communicate directly with the world and polish their image, Ali bent the media of the day to his will through outrageous publicity stunts, quirky poems and memorable catchphrases. Another white-dominated institution, the mainstream media, had to deal with an unprecedented, freewheeling assault on its familiar control routines by a black athlete who refused to be deferent and grateful.

This boxing-related pantomime was entertaining. But it was when the brand new world heavyweight champion rejected his "slave name" in 1964, became Muhammad Ali and declared his allegiance to the black separatist Nation of Islam that he became a major political presence in popular culture.

His subsequent refusal—on religious and ethical grounds—to be conscripted to the US armed forces and to fight in the Vietnam War turned him into both a figure of hate and a symbol of hope in a bitterly divided America. The world beyond boxing and America now had even more reason to pay close attention to Muhammad Ali.

Ali explains his refusal to serve in the US armed forces.

Once more, Ali was ahead of the game. Anticipating the deep political divisions over the two Gulf Wars and their disastrous outcomes, here was a vibrant celebrity around whom dissenters could rally.

Banned from boxing for three years because of his political stance, Ali acquired the status of a martyr to his convictions. He stood conspicuous among fellow sport stars who kept their heads down on matters of politics—whatever their private views.

In retrospect, it is remarkable that he was not assassinated like the Kennedys, Martin Luther King Jr, and Malcolm X.

When he returned to the ring, Ali became the focus of spectacular media-sport events like "The Rumble in the Jungle" and "The Thrilla in Manila". These boxing matches helped write the rule book of 21st-century "sportainment".

Ali's boxing career petered out, yet he remained an instantly recognisable global celebrity. But by 1984 the savage toll that boxing took on his body, especially his brain, became evident. It is believed to have exacerbated the Parkinson's disease that progressively debilitated him.

Some of the most touching and heart-breaking moments in sport came when his shaking body performed ceremonial duties at the 1996 Atlanta and 2012 London Olympics. When Ali spoke in public, his rapid-fire repartee was reduced to a low, slow whisper.

Despite his failing health, Ali relentlessly pursued his humanistic activities. He supported charities and foundations such as Athletes for Hope, UNICEF, and his own Muhammad Ali Center.

Ali was no saint. His cruel mocking of rival Joe Frazier, which he later regretted, saw him treat a fellow African American as a "dumb", "ugly", racially complicit Uncle Tom in a manner that resonated with some of the worst racist stereotypes. His complicated history of intimate relationships with women and his many offspring is of soap-opera proportions.

But, in touching and enhancing the lives of so many people across the globe, here was a man much more sinned against than sinning.

Ali's passing comes at a time of increasing concern about sport-induced traumatic brain injury. The near-fatal outcome of a recent bout in the UK between Nick Blackwell and Chris Eubank Jr has once again put boxing in an unfavourable spotlight.

Ali paid a ferocious price for his fame. Most leading medical associations would ban the sport that brought him to prominence.

Yet, paradoxically, it is boxing that we have to thank for somehow—out of the violence and pain of its self-proclaimed "sweet science" —delivering to the world Muhammad Ali, The People's Champion.

~

"Muhammad Ali rewrote the rule book for athletes as celebrities and activists," David Rowe. This article was originally published on The Conversation.

[TWENTY-FIVE]

How 'The Greatest' Fought War and Racism

By Garikai Chengu

Garikai Chengu is a scholar at Harvard University.

~

Boxing changed American history. The sport of boxing had more to do with the advancement of the civil rights movement than any other sport. From Jack Johnson to Joe Lewis to Muhammad Ali.

Sunday marked the 74th birthday of arguably the greatest and most beloved Black athlete in history: Muhammad Ali.

No sport has exploited athletes, particularly black athletes, quite like boxing. The very first boxers in America were African slaves. White slave owners would amuse themselves by forcing slaves to box to the death while wearing iron collars.

Even after the abolition of slavery, boxing became the first sport to be desegregated so that white boxing promoters could continue to exploit blacks and make money from the deep racism in American society.

Eugenics was used to justified slavery, and the pseudo science of the time "proved" that blacks were not only mentally inferior, but also physically inferior to whites.

Ironically, early white fight promoters unwittingly created a space where black boxers could destroy white supremacist ideas of society and racial hierarchy.

The 1910 victory of Jack Johnson against "The Great White Hope" launched one of the greatest nationwide race riots in US history. Out of that embarrassment, in which a black man defeated a white man, Congress passed a law outlawing boxing films.

With a brief look at the history of boxing, it is abundantly clear that the races and cultures that have suffered the most at any given time always tend to produce the greatest champions.

Boxing has a tendency to both attract and indeed prey upon talent from underprivileged minority communities. Through boxing, one can read a direct chart of underprivilege in America: highlighting which minorities struggle to make it up the ladder, until they succeed and then disappear from the boxing scene; and which minorities are still in the ring, because they are still at the bottom rung of America's societal ladder.

You had the wave of Jewish boxers, then successful Irish boxers, Italian-American boxers, African American boxers, and now, increasingly Hispanic boxers.

In a society that is so violently racist, the sport of boxing became an escape valve for people's anger. Boxing symbolised a twisted manifestation of the American dream, where minorities have to, literally, fight their way out of poverty.

The modern image of Muhammad Ali, portrayed by the establishment, is one of a black man dancing in the ring and shouting "I am the greatest!" His image is now used to sell everything from luxury cars to soft drinks.

Despite the establishment's whitewashing and Santaclausification of Ali's image, history shows that the true Muhammad Ali was a staunch black nationalist, who was good friends with Malcolm X and a member of the Black Power group, The Nation of Islam.

Ali was unquestionably the best boxer in history, not simply because of his achievements in the ring, but because he brought the fight against racism and war into professional sports.

Muhammad Ali grew up in the 1950s and 1960s, as the black freedom struggle was heating up and beginning to boil over. Born in Louisville as Cassius Clay to a house painter and domestic worker, Ali was immersed in America's racist nature from birth.

After winning the Olympic gold medal at the age of 18, Ali was so proud of his medal that he said he wore it round his neck almost all the time. Fellow Olympian W. Rudolph remarked: "He slept with it, he went to the cafeteria with it. He never took it off."

Days after returning from the Olympic Games, Ali was eating in a restaurant with the medal swinging around his neck and he was denied service by the white restaurant owners. Ali then threw the gold medal into the Ohio River.

Ali found answers to America's racism in friend and mentor Malcolm X and the Nation of Islam. "X and Ali were one in the same," journalist J. Tinsley wrote. "Both were young, handsome, intelligent, outspoken African American men who scared the crap out of White America during a time period when racial tension was the norm."

With the Nation of Islam, Ali rejected the name Clay, because black Americans' last names were inherited from their slave masters.

At a time when most of the country were in favour of the Vietnam War, Ali asked: "Why should they ask me to put on a uniform and go 10,000 miles from home and drop bombs and bullets on brown people in Vietnam while so-called Negro people in Louisville are treated like dogs and denied simple human rights? So I'll go to jail, so what? We've been in jail for 400 years."

The typical sentence for refusing to go to war was 18 months, but an all-white jury convicted Ali and he was sentenced to 60 months, or five years, in prison for standing up to America's most violent racism at home and abroad.

Boxing changed American history.

The sport of boxing had more to do with the advancement of

the civil rights movement than any other sport. From Jack Johnson to Joe Lewis to Muhammad Ali.

There ultimately has never been an athlete more vilified by the American press, more persecuted by the US government, or more defiantly beloved across the whole world than Muhammad Ali.

~

"Ali—How 'The Greatest' Fought War and Racism," Garikai Chengu, January 19, 2016. Licensed from allAfrica.com.

[TWENTY-SIX]

Muhammad Ali: A Life in Quotes

By Al Jazeera

In his life, Muhammad Ali taunted opponents with razor-sharp rhymes and comical one-liners. But his quotes on achievement, social justice, religion and war made him an iconic cultural figure. Here are some of his most famous quotes:

On Boxing

"Float like a butterfly, sting like a bee. Rumble, young man, rumble."

— Ali, before a fight with Sonny Liston in 1964.

"I'm king of the world! I'm pretty! I'm a bad man! I shook up the world! I shook up the world! I shook up the world!"

—Ali after beating Liston.

"I've wrestled with alligators, I've tussled with a whale. I done handcuffed lightning. And throw thunder in jail.""You know I'm bad. Just last week, I murdered a rock, injured a stone, hospitalised a brick. I'm so mean, I make medicine sick."

—After his match against George Foreman, known as the Rumble in the Jungle in 1974.

"All I can do is fight for truth and justice. I can't save anybody. He's a science fiction character, and I'm a real character."

—Ali at a news conference to announce a comic book in which he beats Superman.

On Success

"What I suffered physically was worth what I've accomplished in life. A man who is not courageous enough to take risks will never accomplish anything in life."

—Ali at a news conference on October 28, 1984.

"It's hard to be humble when you're as great as I am."

—undated.

"Hey Floyd—I seen you! Someday I'm gonna whup you! Don't you forget, I am the greatest!"

—Ali to heavyweight champion Floyd Patterson during the 1960 Olympic Games.

On War

Muhammad Ali also spoke boldly against the war in Vietnam and refused conscription into the army. This is Ali's famous explanation of why he refused to serve in the United States Army:

"Why should they ask me to put on a uniform and go ten thousand miles from home and drop bombs and bullets on brown people in Vietnam while so-called Negro people in Louisville are treated like dogs and denied simple human rights?"

—Ali, February, 17, 1966.

Muhammad Ali was thus convicted of draft evasion, and the US government tried to send him to prison. But the US Supreme Court later overturned the charges. Muhammad Ali praised God on hearing the news.

"I've done my celebrating already. I said a prayer to Allah."

—Ali, June 28, 1971

"They did what they thought was right, and I did what I thought was right."

On Racism and Islam

Muhammad Ali was an outspoken Muslim convert, and he became the unofficial spokesman for millions of blacks and oppressed people around the world. In Seattle for a benefit for Sugar Ray Seales, he famously said:

"People say I talk so slow today. That's no surprise. I calculated I've taken 29,000 punches. But I earned $57 million and I saved half of it. So I took a few hard knocks. Do you know how many black men are killed every year by guns and knives without a penny to their names? I may talk slow, but my mind is OK."

—Ali, January 20, 1984.

"Why are all the angels white? Why ain't there no black angels?"

—Ali at a church in 1983.

"My name is known in Serbia, Pakistan, Morocco. These are countries that don't follow the Kentucky Derby."

—Ali in a *New York Times interview*, April 1977.

Since the Paris attacks, Muhammad Ali spoke out against the incrimination of Islam with ISIL attacks:

> *"I am a Muslim and there is nothing Islamic about killing innocent people in Paris, San Bernardino, or anywhere else in the world. True Muslims know that the ruthless violence of so called Islamic Jihadists goes against the very tenets of our religion."*
>
> —Ali, 2015.

~

"Muhammad Ali: A life in quotes," June 4, 2016. Licensed from Al Jazeera.

FIGHTING WORDS

[About FanReads]

Founded in 2016, FanReads publishes collections of the greatest stories ever told for fans of sports, screen, music and gaming.

Visit www.fanreads.com to sign up for FanReader, our free weekly digest with the very best writing about sports, screen, music and gaming, delivered straight to your inbox each Monday.

Follow us on Facebook and Twitter for news and special offers.

www.fanreads.com

Twitter: @FanReads

Facebook: FanReads

info@fanreads.com

[More From FanReads]

Sports

Bat Flip: The Greatest Toronto Blue Jays Stories Ever Told

Screen

For the Watch: The Greatest Game of Thrones Stories Ever Told

Music

Long and Winding Road: The Greatest Beatles Stories Ever Told

Gaming

Catch 'Em All: The Greatest Pokemon Go Stories Ever Told

www.fanreads.com

[Join the FanReads Team]

Curators

FanReads is looking for editors to curate fan-based anthologies. If you're a skilled writer / editor, a motivated entrepreneur and a fan of sports, screen or music, we want to hear from you.

Reach out to submissions@fanreads.com with your credentials and potential topics of interest.

Contributors

FanReads is always on the lookout for the very best writing on fan-based themes.

If you've published great content on sports, screen or music and want us to consider your content for republication in a FanReads title, please let us know at submissions@fanreads.com.

submissions@fanreads.com

[About the Editor]

Keith McArthur is President and Publisher of FanReads. His first book, Air Monopoly, was published in 2004. He lives in Toronto with his wife Laura and sons Connor and Bryson.

keith.mcarthur@fanreads.com